INSPIRATIONAL FOOTBALL ST🏈RIES FOR KIDS

LIONEL ANDERSON

ALSO BY THE AUTHOR

Inspirational Soccer Stories For Kids

https://www.champlinks.com/sl/soccer/

Inspirational Hockey Stories For Kids

https://www.champlinks.com/sl/hockey/

Inspirational Basketball Stories For Kids

https://www.champlinks.com/sl/basketball/

CONTENTS

KICKING OFF: THE POWER OF FOOTBALL STORIES

Hey there, dream-chasers! Get ready to step into something absolutely incredible—the heart-pounding, soul-stirring world of football stories that'll have you believing in the impossible!

Imagine a packed stadium, the roar of the crowd, and those magical moments that transform ordinary players into living legends . Think about it—every touchdown, every game-winning play, and every championship victory carries a bigger message that'll fire you up to chase your dreams .

These are more than football stories—they're pure rocket fuel for your spirit!

THE UNIVERSAL LANGUAGE OF FOOTBALL

You know what's wild? Football is like a universal translator for life! No matter where you go, or what language people speak, football connects us all .

In math class? Oh, you better believe it! Those offensive formations are practically teaching geometry in real-time, showing you angles, patterns, and shapes that make the game and math class way cooler . Science? Oh, yeah— every perfect spiral and mind-boggling catch has physics written all over it! You're watching velocity, torque, and momentum in action . Talk about the coolest science experiment ever! Literature? Think about it .Football is packed with the hero's journey, the twists and turns, the excitement, and the victory, all wrapped up in one intense, heart-pounding storyline!

FROM BACKYARD TO SUPERBOWL: CHAMPIONS IN THE MAKING

Let's take a minute to talk about the legends of the game—guys who became household names but started exactly like you, as kids throwing around a ball, with big dreams and bigger goals!

Tom Brady, one of the most decorated players in history, was picked 199th in the draft .That's right, he didn't start at the top—he had to work his way up with determination and perseverance, proving people wrong at every step .Or what about John Madden? He went from a simple football player as a kid to a young coach of the Raiders to become the ultimate name in football, a video game icon, in about every gaming console across the land!

These heroes of the gridiron didn't have it all handed to them .They knew what it meant to stay determined, to feel like an underdog, and to get back up every time they got knocked down .And the best part? They started right where you are now .All kids with dreams, a ball, and the courage to go after it .

Football isn't only about winning games—it's about winning at life! Every fumble you recover from, every mistake you make, and every victory you earn makes you stronger, both on and off the field .Those doubts, those fears that sneak up on you? The greats felt them too .But they kept a confident mindset and overcame them!

They persevered, and so can you!

LESSONS—THE POWER OF INSPIRATION

Let me drop some truth bombs about motivation —it's that fire in your belly that turns "I can't" into "Watch me!" It's that voice in your head saying "You got this! " when your muscles are begging to quit .And these football stories? They're matches ready to light that fire!

These aren't stats and scores we're talking about—they're blueprints for greatness! When you're struggling with that tough algebra problem, remind yourself how Brady analyzed defenses for hours after practice .When you're facing setbacks, look at how Peyton Manning turned those game strategy planning sessions into the greatest plays in NFL history!

Want to really cement these lessons?

Break down your favorite player's path to greatness .What obstacles did they overcome? What habits made them successful? Then boom—create your own game plan for success, whether it's acing that next test or making the varsity team .Check this out—when you read about your hero's dedication, suddenly hitting the books doesn't feel like a chore—it feels like following in the footsteps of greatness! When you learn how your favorite QB bounced back from defeat, that failed quiz becomes nothing more than a first-quarter setback in your own success story!

Here's the real touchdown play—these stories show us that greatness isn't some magical gift bestowed upon the chosen few .It's built into those early-morning workouts, late-night study sessions, and the daily choice to keep pushing when giving up feels like the easier option .

And that's what makes football stories so incredibly powerful—they remind us that every champion started as an underdog, every victory was built on countless setbacks, and every legend began as someone brave enough to dream big .

So let's huddle up and get real—these aren't fairytales we're sharing .They're fuel for the next generation of champions, innovators, and world-changers . Because when you combine the raw passion of football with the power of storytelling, you create something truly magical—your very own playbook for turning your dreams into reality!

Every football legend you admire started exactly where you are right now .The only difference? They decided to write their own story of greatness .And guess what? Your blank pages are waiting—it's time to pick up that pen and start writing your legacy of awesomeness!

The field is yours, and your story? Well, that's gonna be one for the record books! Let's go make it happen!

JOE MADDEN AND PEYTON MANNING

Now, let's take a look at the mind-blowing power of leadership through the eyes of two absolute titans who revolutionized what it means to lead!

When we talk about Joe Madden and Peyton Manning, we're not talking about your average playmakers .No way, pal! These guys took leadership and turned it into an art form that'll have you fired up to become the superstar leader you were born to be!

Let's break it down, starting with the legendary Peyton Manning—talk about a field general! This guy didn't become known as "The Sheriff" by accident . While everyone else was watching game film, Manning was totally *LIVING* it, transforming every single practice into a masterclass in excellence .He didn't wait for greatness to happen—he *CREATED* it, lifting every single player around him to heights they never thought possible! And check this out— Manning didn't stop at making himself better .Nope! He had this incredible gift of making everyone around him step up their game .From rookie receivers to veteran linemen, when you played with Peyton, you weren't playing for the stats—you were playing for greatness!

Now, slide over to Joe Madden, and BAM—you've got another leadership superhero who showed us that being a boss isn't about barking orders—it's about building belief! This guy understood that true leadership isn't about wearing the biggest title or having the loudest voice—it's about creating an environment where everyone feels like an MVP!

Here's the game changer—these leaders didn't limit their impact to the field only . Their leadership style created ripple effects that transformed entire organizations, communities, and yes—even the lives of fans watching from home! That's the thing about real leadership—it breaks through barriers and inspires excellence everywhere it goes! Think about it—when Manning stepped up to the line of scrimmage, he was calling plays and orchestrating excellence! When Madden stepped into the clubhouse, he was igniting each player's full potential! These guys showed us that leadership is a choice to make everyone around you better!

And, YOU can tap into this exact same leadership magic! Whether you're captain of your team, leading a group project, or stepping up in your community, these leadership lessons are your weapon for success!

Want to know the real MVP move?

Start treating every situation like Manning treated every play—as an opportunity to elevate everyone around you .Begin approaching challenges like Madden— with the unwavering belief that your team can achieve the impossible! Remember this—Manning and Madden didn't become legends by following the playbook—they wrote their own! They showed us that true leadership isn't about being in charge—it's about taking charge of making positive change happen!

So what's it gonna be, champions? Are you ready to step up and lead like these legends?

JOHN MADDEN—FROM COACH TO CULTURAL ICON

Let me tell you about a true football legend who'll blow your mind—the one and only John Madden! This story is about a cultural phenomenon that transcends the gridiron and reaches into the very heart of American sports .

Imagine being so incredible at what you do that your name becomes synonymous with football itself .That's exactly what Coach Madden did, and boy, do I have some stories to share with you! This isn't all about Xs and Os— it's about inspiration, innovation, and an unforgettable legacy .First off, let's talk about his coaching days with the Raiders .Now, use your imagination: there's a young coach with a fiery spirit, a booming voice, and a brain that could outthink any opponent on the field .That was Madden! This man didn't just build players—he built believers . His locker room was a forge where confidence, determination, and unbreakable camaraderie were crafted .

His players saw a leader who believed in them even when they doubted themselves .Madden's secret weapon? He had this uncanny ability to make the most complicated football strategies feel as simple as a backyard scrimmage . Need to understand a blitz package? Madden had a metaphor for that . Confused about a zone defense? He'd break it down into something you could explain to your dog .He turned every huddle and chalkboard session into an "Oh WOW!" moment .

And talk about results! In ten seasons with the Raiders, he racked up an unbelievable 759 winning percentage, the best of any coach with over 100 career victories .His crowning achievement? Leading the Raiders to their first Super Bowl victory in 1977 .But more than trophies and titles, Madden gave his players something even greater: the belief that they were unstoppable .When John Madden traded the sidelines for the broadcast booth, the football world didn't know what was about to hit it .Let me tell you, he revolutionized the way we watch football .Before Madden, commentators gave dry play-by-plays that felt more like a weather report than an epic showdown .Madden changed that—he made football *fun* .

Remember those telestrator drawings that lit up your screen during games? The circles, arrows, and zig-zags that turned complex plays into works of art?

That was Madden .He turned a simple tool into an engaging storytelling device, making you feel like you were watching the game with your favorite uncle who happened to know everything about football .He showed you why it mattered, often with a dose of humor and a BOOM! for good measure .

Madden brought football to life in a way that no one had done before .He was like a translator, bridging the gap between hardcore fans and casual viewers . Whether you were a die-hard or a first-timer, Madden made you feel like you belonged in the football family .And let's not forget the voice! That booming, gravelly, passionate voice that could turn a routine screen pass into the most exciting moment of your Sunday .Madden wasn't merely describing the game— he was living it, and he made sure you were right there with him .

Now, let's talk about *Madden NFL,* the video game that became a cultural juggernaut! That's right—the game sitting in millions of living rooms across the world carries his name .And why not? Nobody made football more fun, more accessible, and more exciting than John Madden .

When Electronic Arts approached him in the late 1980s about creating a football video game, Madden had one non-negotiable demand: it had to be real football .Not seven-on-seven, not simplified plays—it had to capture the full complexity and excitement of the NFL .Madden's insistence on authenticity turned what could have been another arcade game into the gold standard for sports simulation .Since its debut in 1988, *Madden NFL* has become a cultural phenomenon, selling over 130 million copies and counting .But it's more than a game—it's an institution .From teaching kids the intricacies of the game to becoming a staple of college dorms and living room tournaments, *Madden NFL* is a rite of passage .And at its core is the same thing that defined Madden himself: a love for football that's contagious .

What made John Madden so special was his relatability . He wasn't the polished, buttoned-up figure you might expect from someone at the top of his field .Madden was real . He was the guy who got as excited about a perfectly executed block as he did about a game-winning touchdown .And let's not forget his love of the bus .That's right—while other commentators flew from city to city, Madden crisscrossed the country in the Madden Cruiser, his custom RV . Why? Because he hated flying and loved connecting with America .On those long road trips, he'd stop at diners, chat with fans, and soak up the culture of the towns he visited .That down-to-earth approach was quintessential Madden .

Madden's larger-than-life personality also made him a natural pitchman . Whether he was endorsing hardware stores or fast food, his enthusiasm was infectious . He sold the idea that life—and football—should be approached with passion and joy .

He didn't only leave a mark on football; he became football . His impact is woven into every facet of the game, from the way it's played to the way it's broadcast to the way it's celebrated in living rooms and stadiums alike . Even after his passing, Madden's legacy continues to thrive . The annual release of *Madden NFL* is still a major event, drawing fans from around the globe . His influence on broadcasting is evident every Sunday, as commentators strive to capture even a fraction of his insight and charisma .

And then there's the John Madden Thanksgiving tradition . Who could forget the "Turkey Leg Award" he created to honor the best players of the Thanksgiving Day games? It was classic Madden—fun, spontaneous, and unforgettable .

At his core, John Madden was a teacher . Whether he was coaching on the sidelines, explaining a play in the booth, or designing a video game, his goal was always the same: to share his love and knowledge of football with the world . He had a unique ability to make the complex simple and the intimidating approachable . Madden wanted you to understand football, to feel the excitement and strategy that made the game so special . He believed that football wasn't only for athletes or experts; it was for everyone . And he dedicated his life to making sure everyone could share in the joy .

John Madden's journey from coach to cultural icon is a story of passion, innovation, and connection . He didn't change football—he changed the way we experience it . He showed us that sports are about more than competition; they're about community, storytelling, and the shared thrill of the game .

So the next time you hear his voice in your head saying, "BOOM!" or find yourself explaining a play like a telestrator wizard, remember the man who made it all possible .John Madden was a game-changer, a legend, a teacher, and a friend to every football fan .

Here's to the coach, the broadcaster, the icon .BOOM!

What a champ!

PEYTON MANNING—THE QUARTERBACK AS A FIELD GENERAL

Let me drop some knowledge about the mastermind of the gridiron—Peyton Manning!

So, it's the fourth quarter, two minutes left, and the defense thinks they've got everything figured out . But wait—there's Manning at the line of scrimmage, pointing, calling out signals, and basically playing chess while everyone else is stuck on checkers! That's what made him "The Sheriff"—he completely OWNED the field! Watching him orchestrate a game was like seeing a maestro conduct a symphony, every movement precise, every call deliberate .You knew something special was about to unfold .

Peyton Manning was the living, breathing definition of football IQ .His mind worked differently from anyone else's .Most players memorized plays; Manning elevated the game into its own form of an intellectual showdown .

Remember "Omaha! Omaha!"?

That wasn't a random shout—it was a code, a strategic masterpiece designed to confuse defenses and keep them guessing . Hearing it meant Peyton was rewriting the script in real time, adjusting to every twitch of the defense like a chess grandmaster predicting moves three steps ahead .

But let's talk about what set Manning apart—his preparation .It's the stuff of legend .While other players were hitting the showers, Manning was in the film room, dissecting defenses like a scientist analyzing the universe .He lived and breathed it .Defensive schemes, individual tendencies, blitz patterns—Manning knew them all, sometimes better than the opposing teams did themselves . Coaches often said Manning prepared as if he were a coach, not just a player, making him arguably the most prepared quarterback in NFL history .

What made him truly remarkable was how he elevated everyone around him . Manning didn't only throw touchdowns; he created stars .He turned average receivers into Pro Bowlers, transformed good teams into juggernauts, and inspired greatness in everyone he worked with .Whether it was the Indianapolis Colts or the Denver Broncos, Peyton carried success with him like a favorite playbook .The Colts became perennial contenders under his leadership, even capturing a Super Bowl in the 2006 season .And when he moved to Denver?

Boom—another Super Bowl victory, this time in the 2015 season, cementing his legacy with two championship rings and countless unforgettable moments .

Let's not forget his leadership style .Manning led with his mind, his heart, and an unrelenting work ethic .He wasn't the guy screaming in your face; he was the guy setting the bar so high that you couldn't help but rise to meet it .First one in, last one out—that was Manning .He made his teammates better by his incredible performances on the field and the example he set every single day .It wasn't about ego; it was about excellence .Even off the field, Peyton continued to impress . His comedic timing in commercials, especially for companies like Nationwide and Gatorade, showcased a self-aware charm that made him relatable to fans everywhere .Whether breaking down game film or delivering hilarious one-liners, Manning proved he was a football icon and a cultural icon, too .

The numbers, of course, speak for themselves .Over an 18-year career, Peyton threw for over 71,000 yards and 539 touchdowns, earning five NFL MVP awards—the most by any player in history .He set the single-season records for passing yards and touchdowns in 2013 with the Broncos, a year that epitomized his greatness .These are more than statistics; they're monuments to a career defined by the relentless pursuit of perfection .

After retirement, he transitioned seamlessly into new roles, from hosting "Peyton's Places" on ESPN+ to mentoring younger players . Manning has become a sort of elder statesman of football, someone whose opinion carries weight and whose presence continues to elevate the sport .

And let's circle back to that iconic phrase—"Omaha ." It's become so synonymous with Manning's legacy in pop culture . Businesses in Omaha, Nebraska, even reported a spike in exposure and sales thanks to his playful use of the term .That's the kind of influence Manning had—turning even his audibles into cultural phenomena .

If you're thinking this is just a story about football, think again .

Manning's journey is a lesson in excellence, preparation, and leadership . Whether you're dreaming of being a quarterback, leading a team, or excelling in your field, Manning's story offers a playbook for success .His dedication to his craft, his ability to inspire others, and his relentless quest for greatness are qualities that transcend sports .

So here's the takeaway: greatness is about more than having talent; it's about what you do with it .It's about the hours you put in when no one's watching, the commitment to your team, and the drive to be better than you were yesterday . Peyton Manning showed us that success is crafted, one deliberate decision at a time .

And now, the ball's in your court .Whether you're calling plays like Manning or inspiring others to reach their potential, remember—you've got the tools to create something extraordinary .These legends didn't succeed because they were special .They became special because they never stopped believing, learning, and growing .

So take a page out of Manning's playbook, and let's see what incredible things you'll accomplish!

LESSON—THE IMPORTANCE OF STRATEGIC THINKING AND LEADERSHIP

Ready to unlock the incredible secrets of leadership that'll transform you into an absolute game-changer? Let's power up with some mind-blowing wisdom from our football heroes!

This is where everything changes! Leadership isn't about being the loudest voice in the room or wearing the captain's badge—it's about combining brilliant strategy with amazing people skills to create something magical!

And boy, did Madden and Manning show us how it's done!

Think of leadership like being a master chef in the kitchen of success—you need both the perfect recipe (that's your strategy) *AND* the ability to bring out the best in your cooking team (that's your people skills)! When you mix these ingredients together? BAM! You've got a recipe for pure excellence!

Let's break down how our legends mastered this mix:

- **John Madden's Leadership Recipe**
  - Turned complex plays into simple, winning strategies
  - Created an environment where every player felt like an MVP
  - Built trust through honest communication
  - Made everyone feel part of something bigger than themselves
- **Peyton Manning's Success Sauce**
  - Read situations like a master detective
  - Adapted plans on the fly when needed
  - Lifted teammates to new levels of excellence
  - Led by example with incredible preparation

Now, here's where it gets super exciting—*YOU* can develop these same incredible skills! Check out these power moves you can start using today:

1. **The Strategic Mastermind Playbook**
   a. Before group projects, map out everyone's strengths (Manning-style!)
   b. Create clear game plans with backup options
   c. Learn to read situations and adjust your approach
   d. Practice making quick, smart decisions

2. **The People Skills Power Up**

   a . Listen to your teammates like Madden listened to his players

   b . Celebrate others' wins (big AND small!)

   c . Build trust through consistent support

   d . Make everyone feel valued and heard

3. **The Daily Leadership Challenge**

   a . Look for chances to help others shine

   b . Step up when challenges arise

   c . Share knowledge and lift others up

   d . Be the positive energy your team needs

Here's some real-world magic you can create with these skills:

- **In the Classroom**
  - Turn group projects into championship opportunities
  - Help struggling classmates understand tough concepts
  - Create study groups where everyone contributes
  - Build an atmosphere where questions are welcomed and celebrated

- **In Sports**
  - Be the teammate who brings energy to practice
  - Help new players feel welcome and supported
  - Share tips and techniques you've mastered
  - Stay positive when things get tough

- **In Life**
  - Empower yourself and others
  - Include others who might feel left out
  - Share your knowledge and skills
  - Be someone others can count on

But here's the real touchdown play—these skills aren't locked in a trophy case somewhere! They're living, breathing superpowers you can use every single day!

When you see someone struggling with homework? BAM! That's your chance to be like Manning, breaking down complex problems into simple solutions! When you notice a teammate feeling down? BOOM! Channel your inner Madden and lift their spirits with encouragement and support! Remember this golden nugget of truth: leadership isn't about being perfect—it's about making others better! Every time you help someone solve a problem, every time you speak up for someone who needs support, every time you bring positive energy to a tough situation—you're not thinking like a leader, you ARE a leader!

And, the positive changes you create through leadership? They're like throwing a perfect spiral into a pond—the ripples keep spreading! When you lead with heart and smarts, you inspire others to do the same .Before you know it, you've created a whole team of leaders who are out there making the world better!

So what's the final score on leadership?

It's not about the titles or the spotlight—it's about making a positive difference every chance you get!

Remember—you've got everything you need right now to start making a difference! Your teammates, classmates, friends, and family are waiting for your unique brand of leadership magic!

Your time to shine is NOW, champion!

HEY SPORTS FANS!

I wanted to say welcome to this world of Inspirational Sports Stories for Kids!

As a thank you for becoming one of our readers, I've put together some amazing gifts for you.

By scanning the QR code or clicking the link (If you are reading the eBook) below, you will gain access to:

- **Positive Mindset for Young Champions** — Master the mental game and train your brain like a pro.
- **Sports Snapshots: Fun Facts for Young Champions** — Discover amazing and unexpected facts about the sports you love.
- **Tracking Score Journal** — For Tracking Scores in 4 different sports!

So go ahead and scan this QR code and take your love for sports to the next level.

Lionel

Keep playing, keep dreaming, and always have fun!

https://stan.store/LionelAnderson/p/sports-snapshots-fun-facts-for-young-champions-rkb37s5w

TOM BRADY AND JOHN ELWAY

I'm about to take you on the ultimate ride through one of the most powerful lessons you'll ever learn—the power of resilience and determination!

In the wild world of football, the true champions aren't the ones who coast to victory. Nah, the real MVPs are the ones who stare adversity right in the face and say, "Is that all you got?" Because let me tell you, some of the most electrifying moments in this sport happen when a team or a player is down, but definitely not out. Those comebacks, my friends, those are the moments that have the power to rock your world!

But why does this matter, you ask?

Well, the ability to persevere, to never give up, to keep fighting no matter what life throws your way—that's a life skill .Because let's be real, the road to success, whether on the gridiron, in the classroom, or your dream job, isn't always smooth sailing .There are gonna be ups and downs, twists and turns, and the only way to make it through is to have that unbreakable spirit, that fire that burns brighter the harder things get .And you know who's got that kind of mindset in spades? The football legends, that's who! These are the players who've stared down the toughest challenges, who've been counted out more times than they can count, and yet, they still find a way to come out on top . Why? Because they know that the true measure of a champion isn't how far you fall, it's how high you bounce back .

So let's take a look at some of these football heroes and see what we can learn .Because the lessons they've got to share are gonna light a fire under you that'll have you ready to take on the world .We're talking about the kind of determination that can turn a game, a career, heck, even a life around in an instant .The kind of resilience that'll have you bouncing back stronger than ever, no matter what curveballs come your way .

And the best part?

These aren't just football skills, my friends . Nope, the mindset required for those epic comebacks, that unwavering belief in yourself, that relentless drive to succeed—that's something you can apply to every single aspect of your life . Whether you're tackling a tough assignment, navigating the ups and downs of a new job, or even trying to navigate the craziness of growing up, this ability to never give up, to keep pushing forward no matter what is gonna be your secret weapon .

TOM BRADY—FROM LATE-ROUND DRAFT PICK TO GOAT

Do you want an uplifting and inspirational story about Tom Brady's journey from a late-round draft pick to the undisputed GOAT? You got it!

Let's rewind the clock to the year 2000, a time when a young quarterback out of Michigan named Tom Brady was sitting anxiously by the phone, waiting to hear his name called in the NFL Draft .Now, this kid was no slouch—he'd had a solid college career, including a clutch performance in the 2000 Orange

Bowl .But in the eyes of NFL scouts? He wasn't flashy, wasn't fast, and didn't have the cannon arm of some of his peers .When his name was finally called as the 199th overall pick by the New England Patriots, it was less of a headline and more of a footnote .A sixth-round pick, barely a blip on the radar .Most people didn't expect much from him .

But here's the thing about Tom Brady: he THRIVES on being underestimated .

From the moment he stepped into the Patriots' training camp, Brady had one thing on his mind: proving everyone wrong .His famous introduction to Patriots owner Robert Kraft was simple but powerful: "I'm the best decision this organization has ever made." Bold, sure . But as history shows, Brady wasn't exaggerating .What separated him from the pack was his relentless work ethic, his laser focus, and a drive to succeed so intense it could power a city .

In his second season, fate stepped in .Starting quarterback Drew Bledsoe went down with an injury, and Brady got his shot .He didn't only fill in—he took over .By the time the playoffs rolled around, he was holding the fort and he was leading the charge .Then came Super Bowl XXXVI, against the heavily favored St .Louis Rams, aka "The Greatest Show on Turf." This was Brady's moment to shine, and shine he did .Cool under pressure, he orchestrated a game-winning drive that ended with Adam Vinatieri's iconic field goal as time expired .The Patriots were champions, and a legend was born .

And that was merely the beginning .

Fast-forward to 2017, Super Bowl LI .The Patriots were trailing the Atlanta Falcons by 25 points late in the third quarter .At that point, most quarterbacks—and most teams—would've folded .But not Brady .No way .With a calmness that belied the gravity of the situation, he led the Patriots to the greatest comeback in Super Bowl history .Play by play, pass by pass, he chipped away at the Falcons' lead until the game was tied .In overtime, Brady sealed the deal, completing a historic victory that still leaves fans and analysts shaking their heads in awe .

But what truly sets Brady apart is his mindset .This is a guy who never rests on his laurels .Seven Super Bowl wins? Cool .He's already thinking about the next one .Five Super Bowl MVPs? Great, but he's still reviewing game films like he's fighting for a roster spot .His diet, his training, his recovery—every aspect of his life is meticulously crafted to keep him at the top of his game .This is discipline, more than mere talent . It's obsession . It's a masterclass in how to turn good into great and great into legendary .

Even when Brady made the leap from the Patriots to the Tampa Bay Buccaneers in 2020, at an age when most players are well into retirement, he didn't miss a beat . In his very first season with the Bucs, he led them to a Super Bowl victory, proving to everyone that his greatness wasn't tied to a single system or team . It was his . And his alone .

Here's another thing that makes Brady special: he's a leader . Watch any footage of him on the sidelines, and you'll see it . He's not giving orders alone—he's rallying his team, firing them up, making them believe they can achieve the impossible . It's no accident that players and coaches who work with him often describe the experience as career-defining . He raises the bar for everyone around him, not by demanding respect but by earning it through his actions and unwavering commitment . Off the field, Brady's journey is also remarkable . Whether it's his role as a family man, his ventures into entrepreneurship, or his TB12 health brand, he's a model of how to channel your success into something meaningful . He's used his platform to celebrate his own achievements and also inspire others to pursue greatness in their own lives .

And let's talk about resilience . Brady's career hasn't been without its setbacks . But none of it has stopped him . If anything, it's fueled him . Every challenge, every obstacle, every time someone said he couldn't, Brady responded the same way: by showing up, working harder, and proving them wrong . Again and again .

But this story is bigger than the name Tom Brady . It's about what he represents . It's about the kid who gets picked last but refuses to give up . It's about the underdog who turns doubters into believers . It's about what's possible when talent meets tenacity, when preparation meets opportunity, and when belief meets action .

Because here's the truth: Brady's story could be anyone's story .

No, we're not all destined to win Super Bowls or shatter NFL records, but we all face moments when the odds are against us when we feel overlooked or underestimated . What matters isn't where you start—it's where you finish . And Brady's journey is living proof that with enough hard work, dedication, and self-belief, you can defy expectations and rewrite the narrative .

So, the next time you feel like the deck is stacked against you, think about that 199th draft pick sitting in his family's living room, wondering if his NFL dream would ever come true. Think about the countless hours he spent working, studying, and preparing. Think about the comebacks, the championships, the sheer willpower it took to become the greatest of all time. And then remember this: you've got that same spark inside you. Brady didn't let his draft position define him, and you don't have to let life's challenges define you. Whether it's in your career, your personal life, or your biggest dreams, you have the power to rise above, to push through, and to create your own legacy.

So, what are you waiting for? The clock's ticking, the game's on the line, and the ball's in your hands.

JOHN ELWAY—THE MASTER OF FOURTH-QUARTER COMEBACKS

John Elway – a name synonymous with grit, greatness, and the relentless pursuit of victory. In the high-octane, gladiator-like world of NFL football, few players could stir up the kind of late-game magic that this Denver Broncos icon consistently delivered.

Whether it was under the blinding lights of playoff intensity or in the cauldron of regular season drama, Elway's unflinching determination and unparalleled poise made him a force of nature in the moments that mattered most. If there's one phrase that could encapsulate Elway's career, it would undoubtedly be "master of fourth-quarter comebacks."

Perhaps no moment epitomizes Elway's brilliance better than what's known as *"The Drive"*. Let's set the stage: It's January 1987, the AFC Championship Game against the Cleveland Browns. The Broncos are pinned at their own two-yard line with only 5:32 remaining on the clock, trailing 20-13. For most quarterbacks, this scenario would induce sheer panic. For Elway, it was a challenge, a puzzle to solve. With laser precision, unshakable calm, and the confidence of a seasoned commander, he orchestrated a 98-yard march down the field. Every throw, every decision, every second was a masterclass in clutch performance. By the time he hit Mark Jackson for a five-yard touchdown pass to tie the game, the stadium buzzed with the electricity of witnessing history in the making. That moment alone vaulted Elway into the pantheon of NFL legends. But here's the thing: *"The Drive"* wasn't an anomaly. It was the blueprint.

Throughout his illustrious career, Elway made a habit of turning impossible situations into triumphant outcomes. He led 35 fourth-quarter comebacks and 46 game-winning drives during his 16-season tenure—a testament to his unyielding will and unmatched ability to thrive under pressure. It wasn't just about the arm strength, though he had one of the most powerful and accurate cannons in NFL history.

No, what set Elway apart was his mental fortitude.

He thrived in chaos, treating every setback as a stepping stone rather than a stumbling block. Whether it was finding a seam in an unrelenting defense, evading sacks with Houdini-like escapability, or inspiring his teammates with fiery determination, Elway always found a way to seize the moment.

But greatness isn't forged in a vacuum, and Elway's journey was anything but smooth. For much of his career, the narrative surrounding him was one of near misses. He led the Broncos to three Super Bowls in the 1980s, only to fall short each time. Those defeats stung, for the fans and for Elway himself, whose competitive fire burned hotter than ever. Lesser players might have crumbled under the weight of those crushing losses, but Elway used them as fuel. He didn't retreat; he retooled. He didn't sulk; he studied. He became a better leader, a more complete quarterback, and an even more formidable competitor.

Elway's persistence paid off in the twilight of his career when everything finally came together. In 1997, at the age of 37—an age when most quarterbacks are eyeing retirement—he led the Broncos to their first Super Bowl victory.

The opponent?

The heavily favored Green Bay Packers, led by the legendary Brett Favre. Elway left an indelible mark on it with his iconic "Helicopter Play." Scrambling for a crucial first down, Elway launched himself into the air, taking a punishing hit but securing the yardage his team needed. It was a moment that perfectly encapsulated his career—a fearless dive into the unknown, driven by an unrelenting desire to win. The Broncos emerged victorious, and Elway finally hoisted the Lombardi Trophy, wiping clean the slate of past failures.

And he wasn't done yet. The very next season, Elway and the Broncos repeated as champions, defeating the Atlanta Falcons in Super Bowl XXXIII. This time, it wasn't just about guts and grit—it was a masterclass in quarterbacking .Elway threw for 336 yards and a touchdown, earning Super Bowl MVP honors in what would be the final game of his career .Talk about going out on top .

Yet, numbers and accolades only tell part of the story .Elway's legacy is about so much more than stats or trophies .It's about the intangibles—the leadership, the resilience, the never-say-die attitude that inspired his teammates and captivated fans .Time and again, he showed that football is as much a mental game as it is a physical one .He had the rare ability to elevate those around him, to make them believe that no deficit was too large and no opponent too formidable .His teammates played with him; they fought for him, and they fed off his unshakable confidence and fiery passion .

Off the field, as a general manager and executive for the Broncos, he brought the same drive and determination to build championship-caliber teams .Under his leadership, Denver claimed another Super Bowl title in 2016, proving that Elway's football genius transcended the playing field .But perhaps more importantly, he became a symbol of perseverance and excellence—a reminder that greatness isn't just about talent but about heart, grit, and the refusal to quit .

When we look back at John Elway's career, it's impossible not to be inspired .

Here was a player who faced immense pressure, staggering setbacks, and relentless scrutiny, yet never wavered in his pursuit of greatness .He taught us that failure isn't the end—it's a step on the path to success .He showed us that true leadership is about more than words; it's about actions, about setting an example and rallying others to achieve the extraordinary .

So, take a page from the John Elway playbook .Embrace the pressure .Relish the opportunity .Attack the problem with the same fearless determination that turned a 98-yard drive into an immortal piece of NFL lore .

No matter how steep the odds, no matter how daunting the challenge, greatness is always within reach for those who refuse to give up .

LESSON—RESILIENCE AND DETERMINATION

Resilience and determination are essential qualities that define the greatest athletes and leaders .Football legends like Tom Brady and John Elway embodied these traits, overcoming adversity to achieve remarkable success .

Brady refused to let his late-round draft status limit him . He channeled perceived slights into relentless self-improvement, leading the Patriots to unprecedented victories .Even when facing a 25-point deficit in Super Bowl LI, Brady engineered a historic comeback, refusing to give up .Elway also excelled at late-game heroics, earning a reputation as the "Master of Fourth-Quarter Comebacks ." Whether engineering "The Drive" or other game-winning moments, Elway inspired his teammates to believe the impossible was possible .

Resilience is the ability to bounce back from setbacks and adapt in the face of challenges .Determination is the unwavering drive to succeed despite obstacles . To cultivate these qualities:

1. **Embrace a growth mindset, believing abilities can be developed through hard work.**

   - Imagine you're a gamer leveling up your character . Maybe you're not great at solving puzzles yet, but with each attempt, you gain XP (experience points) . You're not stuck at "Level Can't Do It" forever; you're in training mode .Keep practicing, and soon, you'll unlock "Level Puzzle Master ."

2. **Reframe challenges as opportunities for learning and improvement.**

   - Got stuck trying to learn how to skateboard? That's not failure; that's a plot twist .With every tumble is the universe saying, "Alright, now let's see how creative you can get with this ." Treat each fall like a clue in your mission to become the next skateboarding superhero .

3. **Build a support network of encouraging friends, family, and mentors.**

   - Think of your friends, family, and mentors as your very own squad in an adventure game . Each teammate brings a special power: maybe one's great at cheering you on, another always has the best advice, and someone else makes you laugh when you're down .You don't need to fight life's big battles alone .

4. **Celebrate small wins to maintain motivation.**

   - Did you finally solve that tricky math problem or get through a tough practice? Cue the confetti! Even superheroes stop to celebrate saving one city before moving on to save the next .Treat yourself to a high-five, a dance break, or maybe a day at the beach or pool —because you earned it .

5. **Visualize overcoming obstacles and achieving goals.**

   - Close your eyes and picture this: You're standing at the base of a giant mountain, and at the top is your dream .Now, imagine yourself climbing, step by step, no matter how hard it gets .You see yourself reaching the summit and shouting, "I did it!" That's your brain doing mental push-ups to get stronger .Keep that vision in your back pocket for when things get tough .

Applying these strategies can help you develop the resilience and determination that fueled Brady, Elway, and other football greats .As Brady said, "Adversity is a gift—an opportunity to grow and get better ."

With that mindset, there's no limit to what you can accomplish .

JERRY RICE AND TRAVIS KELCE

WHOA! Want to know the most INCREDIBLE secret about becoming a champion?! It's all about that GROWTH MINDSET—and football is going to show us how!

You know those amazing catches and mind-blowing plays you see on TV? They weren't born overnight! Every single superstar started with dropping passes and wobbly throws . But here's what makes them special—they saw every fumble as a chance to get better! Think about Jerry Rice, the greatest receiver ever! Did you know he caught 100 balls every day after practice?! While others headed home, he was out there grinding, rain or shine .That's what scientists call a growth mindset—believing you can get better, stronger, and smarter with practice!

But check this out—your brain is like a muscle! The more you challenge it, the stronger it gets! When you practice those spiral throws or route-running, you're actually rewiring your brain to become more awesome! Scientists discovered that every time you practice, your brain builds new connections, making you faster and better at whatever you're working on! Tom Brady wasn't born throwing perfect passes .He started as a backup quarterback who barely made the team! But his secret weapon? He treated every single practice like a Super Bowl game .Every mistake was a chance to learn, every setback an opportunity to come back stronger!

Want to know what's super cool about having a growth mindset? It works everywhere! Those same brain-boosting powers that help you perfect your touchdown dance? They're the exact same ones that help you tackle tough math problems or master a new video game!

Let's break down the awesome power of practice:

- Your brain actually grows new connections when you practice
- Every mistake is like a secret clue showing you where to improve
- Small improvements stack up into massive wins over time
- Consistency beats talent when talent doesn't practice

Remember how we talked about catching 100 balls a day? That's what experts call "atomic habits"—tiny actions that add up to huge results! It's like building a touchdown machine, one play at a time!

Think about it—if you improve by even 1% each day, you'll be 365% better in a year! That's how legends are made! They don't try to change everything at once . They pick ONE thing, crush it with practice, then move to the next!

Here's what makes practice so powerful:

1. It builds your confidence like a fortress

2. It turns tough challenges into exciting opportunities

3. It shows you that YOU control your improvement

4. It proves that champions aren't born - they're BUILT!

The coolest part? Every NFL superstar started at the beginning! They dropped passes, threw wobbly balls, and missed tackles . But they had that growth mindset—they knew every practice was making them stronger!

Remember this: Your brain is ready to grow, your skills are ready to soar, and your future is waiting to be awesome! Every practice, every rep, every single effort is building your path to greatness! So next time practice feels tough, remember—you're not tired, you're getting stronger! You're not struggling, you're growing! And you're not failing, you're learning how to WIN!

That's the power of a growth mindset—it turns every challenge into a chance to become more amazing! Whether you're aiming for the end zone or the honor roll, that mindset will help you score big in everything you do!

That's what makes football so incredible—it's not about being perfect, it's about getting better every single day!

JERRY RICE—THE POWER OF RELENTLESS TRAINING

Jerry Rice—the name alone conjures images of excellence, discipline, and sheer dominance in the NFL .His career was remarkable; a monument to the power of relentless training and unshakable determination .

Let's break down the saga of Jerry Rice, the greatest receiver to ever play the game, and how his commitment to perfection turned him into a legend .

Before Rice became the king of the gridiron, he was a kid growing up in Crawford, Mississippi, catching bricks for his dad, a mason .Bricks, you ask? Yes, BRICKS! While other kids were tossing around footballs, Jerry was developing hands of steel and laser-sharp reflexes by catching those heavy blocks, and helping his dad with his work .Without knowing it, he was laying the foundation for the career to come—literally and figuratively .Those early lessons taught him the value of hard work and precision, qualities that would define his future .

When Rice entered the NFL, the league had already seen some incredible athletes, but Rice was different . He didn't rely solely on his natural talent (though he had plenty) .Instead, he committed to outworking everyone .While other players trained during the season and coasted in the off-season, Rice transformed the term "training" into an art form .He prepared for greatness . And the cornerstone of that preparation? His now-legendary hill workouts . Imagine a 2 5-mile trail so steep it might as well have been Mount Everest .

Rice didn't only jog it—he sprinted it, over and over again, ten times a session . The hill became his sanctuary, his crucible, where he forged the stamina and explosiveness that left defenders gasping in his wake .This wasn't an occasional drill—it was his routine, the relentless grind that separated him from everyone else .

Rice's training regimen didn't stop at the hill .Oh no .His daily schedule was a masterclass in commitment .He'd wake up before the sun, when most people were still dreaming, and attack the day with the intensity of a playoff game . Perfecting his routes? Check .Catching at least 100 passes a day? Absolutely . Hitting the weight room with a gladiator-like focus? You better believe it .And when you thought he might rest, he'd head back to the field to practice more routes, fine-tune his mechanics, and study game film like he was prepping for a doctoral thesis in football .

This wasn't merely about physical preparation—it was about mental domination .Every rep, every sprint, every film session sharpened Rice's football IQ .He turned studying defensive schemes into an obsession, understanding what his opponents were doing and why they were doing it .This gave him an almost psychic ability to read defenses and adjust on the fly, leaving defensive coordinators pulling their hair out .

Rice's obsession with precision extended to every detail of his craft . While many receivers ran their routes with a bit of slack, Rice ran every single one at full speed, as if the game was on the line .He drilled his footwork with the precision of a ninja and practiced catches from every possible angle .He turned perfect form into second nature so that when game day arrived, he executed . And that execution was poetry in motion .

His work ethic paid dividends that most athletes can only dream of .Let's talk numbers—because Rice's stats are the stuff of legend:

- 1,549 receptions, more than anyone in NFL history .That's like catching 100 passes every season for 15 years straight .

- 22,895 receiving yards .To put that in perspective, that's the equivalent of running the length of 229 football fields!

- 208 touchdowns, a record so absurd it's closer to fantasy than reality .

- 13 Pro Bowl selections, more than most players could hope for in two lifetimes .

What's even more incredible is how Rice sustained this level of excellence over two decades .Most players retire before 30 years of age, but Rice defied Father Time .While most receivers see a steep decline after their prime years, Rice kept going, seemingly immune to the laws of aging .At 40 years old, he was still torching defenders and racking up yards like a man half his age .

But Rice's greatness wasn't all about numbers or longevity—it was about the example he set .Even when he was universally acknowledged as the best, he trained like he was fighting for a roster spot .First to practice, last to leave, always running extra routes, always studying more film .His teammates couldn't help but be inspired .How could they not, when the best player in the game was outworking everyone?

What made Rice truly special was his mindset .While others viewed practice as a chore, Rice saw it as a privilege .He didn't have to train—he got to train .He treated every day as an opportunity to improve, to push the boundaries of what was possible .And in doing so, he redefined what it meant to be a professional athlete .

Rice's career is a masterclass in the principles of greatness:

- Excellence isn't built on one big moment; it's the result of thousands of small ones, progressing to the next .
- Champions are made in the shadows when no one's watching .
- Details matter—every step, every catch, every decision .
- Hard work beats talent when talent doesn't work hard .

Rice lived these principles .And in doing so, he showed us all what's possible when talent meets relentless effort .His story is a testament to the idea that greatness isn't handed to anyone—it's earned, one dedicated day at a time .

Even now, long after his playing days are over, Rice's legacy continues to inspire .He's a reminder that success isn't about being the biggest, fastest, or strongest—it's about having the heart, the discipline, and the grit to outwork everyone .So, the next time you're tempted to take a shortcut, remember Jerry Rice sprinting that hill .The next time you feel like you've done enough, think about Rice running extra routes to keep getting better .

Because that's what champions do .They push beyond the limits of what's comfortable .They work when others rest .They chase perfection, knowing they might never catch it but that the pursuit itself is what makes them great .

Jerry Rice set the standard . And in doing so, he gave us all a blueprint for success . Whether you're on the field, in the office, or chasing your own dreams, the lesson is the same: greatness isn't about what you're given . It's about what you're willing to earn . And Jerry Rice earned it all, one hill, one route, and one moment at a time .

TRAVIS KELCE—EVOLVING INTO AN ELITE TIGHT END

INCREDIBLE ALERT! Travis Kelce's journey from high school quarterback to one of the most dominant tight ends in NFL history is the stuff of legends, and it's proof that the impossible is possible if you're willing to put in the work .

Let's check out how Kelce reinvented himself, shattered records, and fundamentally changed what it means to play the tight end position in the NFL .

Did you know that Travis Kelce was once a quarterback in high school?

Yeah, that's right . Before he was running intricate routes and wowing fans, Kelce was throwing the ball himself . But rather than clinging to the comfort of his previous position, he embraced the challenge of becoming something completely new . When his coaches suggested a switch to tight end, it could have been easy to resist or fall back on what he knew . But Kelce saw it as an opportunity to redefine himself and evolve into something extraordinary .

Not knowing the first thing about blocking?

No big deal . Kelce was determined to learn, to push himself beyond what was expected . He dove into every aspect of the position: from blocking techniques to route running, and of course, catching passes . Kelce was far from content with simply being serviceable—he wanted to be exceptional . And that relentless drive paid off in ways that still blow minds today . This transformation didn't happen overnight . Kelce didn't magically become a superstar . No, he put in hours and hours of work that, even now, continue to shape him into a player that defenses dread to face . Every season, Kelce comes back with something new that leaves defenders scratching their heads . From new moves to improved agility, his evolution has been nothing short of phenomenal .

The key to Kelce's success is the way he approaches his training . Every day is a chance to innovate, to perfect a skill, and to push his limits . His morning routine is legendary . It starts with hours of film study, dissecting defensive schemes, and searching for new ways to get open . While most players might only focus on their strengths, Kelce is laser-focused on improving his weaknesses .If catching passes from every angle wasn't enough, he then heads to the field for extra drills .These aren't your run-of-the-mill passing drills either; Kelce is making impossible catches look routine—honing his ability to pluck the ball from the air in the most unconventional ways, from difficult angles, under pressure, or with defenders draped all over him .

And let's talk about blocking .If there's one area that might have posed the biggest challenge for Kelce, it was learning how to block effectively .But as he's done throughout his career, Kelce attacked this challenge head-on .He worked alongside offensive linemen, learning the intricacies of blocking from some of the best in the business .It didn't matter if he wasn't a lineman himself—Kelce understood the value of learning from those who knew the art of controlling the line of scrimmage .His blocking techniques, which rival the skill set of offensive linemen, make him a complete player .

You don't just have to worry about him catching passes down the field; you have to respect his ability to hold his own in the trenches as well .

But it's not just about the raw strength and size of blocking—it's about precision, footwork, and timing .And this is where Kelce's transition to tight end really shines .His route running has evolved into something spectacular, as he's built his own unique blend of precision, agility, and unpredictability . Kelce's ability to create separation, and to get open at will, is what sets him apart from other tight ends and puts him on a pedestal with the best of the best .He combines a wide receiver's footwork with the strength of a tight end, making it incredibly tricky for defenders to overcome him .His routes are so sharp, so perfectly executed, that he makes seasoned defensive backs look lost in coverage .It's no wonder that he's had eight straight seasons with over 1,000 yards—an unheard-of achievement for a tight end .

Even after all this success, Kelce never stops evolving .He has an uncanny ability to innovate, and it's clear that he never rests on his laurels .Every season, you see new tricks, new moves, new ways of getting open .His arsenal is constantly expanding, keeping defenders guessing and coaches scrambling for answers . His work ethic is built on the idea that no matter how much success you achieve, there's always more to learn, and always room to grow .

Kelce's commitment to getting better extends to his entire approach to the game. He's constantly studying, observing, and learning from others. He spends time with wide receivers, picking up their tricks of the trade. He even studies basketball moves to improve his footwork, borrowing techniques from a sport completely different from football. Kelce's training is a mix of old-school toughness with new-school innovation. He's not afraid to combine skills from different positions, making him more versatile and unpredictable with each passing year. Kelce's success is about his willingness to approach the game from all angles, to look at what's been done, and then take it to the next level.

One of the coolest aspects of Kelce's journey is how much he shares with others. He doesn't hoard his knowledge or keep his tips to himself. He learns from veterans, helps rookies get better, and has developed a culture of learning and growth. Whether he's swapping techniques with offensive linemen or challenging younger tight ends to push their limits, Kelce is fostering an environment of continuous improvement. It's about more than his own success—it's about helping everyone around him grow, too.

And that's exactly why Kelce has been able to stay ahead of the curve for so long. The NFL is a constantly changing league, with new defensive schemes and emerging players popping up all the time. But Kelce adapts faster than anyone. He never assumes he has everything figured out—each season brings new challenges, and new opportunities to innovate, and he seizes them all. Innovation isn't a once-in-a-while thing for Kelce—it's a daily habit, a constant part of his routine.

And that's why he continues to be one of the most dangerous and effective players on the field.

The numbers back up everything we're saying. Eight straight seasons with 1,000+ yards?

Unheard of for a tight end. But it's the way Kelce makes his plays look easy. His ability to turn the toughest catches into routine grabs, his smooth route running, and his strength in the blocking game make him one of the most complete players to ever play the position. He combines power with finesse, blending old-school toughness with new-school style. He's always creating mismatches, making defenses uncomfortable no matter where he lines up on the field.

Every week, Kelce's improvement plan is clear . He works to perfect one new route each week, he masters a new blocking technique monthly, and he's constantly adding new moves to his repertoire to beat coverage . His chemistry with his quarterbacks continues to grow stronger, as he fine-tunes his timing and instincts . And no matter what, Kelce always finds creative ways to get open, to make plays, to deliver .

Travis Kelce's evolution is living proof of the idea that greatness doesn't come from staying the same . It comes from embracing change, from challenging yourself to be better, and from practicing relentlessly . His story shows that versatility opens doors, that challenges spark revolutions, and that creativity is the key to greatness . Kelce dominated change . And his journey reminds us all that growth never stops . Success demands adaptation, and excellence comes from the relentless pursuit of improvement .

So, turn challenges into opportunities, setbacks into comebacks, and obstacles into steps toward greatness . Because if Kelce can evolve into the best tight end the NFL has ever seen, then there's no limit to what we can all achieve when we're willing to grow .

Just like him, we can take the unexpected and turn it into something extraordinary .

LESSON—THE VALUE OF CONSISTENT HARD WORK

Let's unlock the ultimate secret that turns everyday players into superstars up close. Yes, you've guessed it, it's all about that SUPER-CHARGED consistent practice!

Remember that our brains are like power-up stations in video games! Every time you practice something—BAM!—your brain builds new superhighways of skill! Dr.Carol Dweck calls this the growth mindset, and it's like having a secret weapon for success!

Check out these mind-blowing facts about practice:

- Your brain creates new connections EVERY TIME you practice
- Small improvements stack up into MASSIVE wins
- Focused practice for 20 minutes beats mindless practice for 2 hours
- Your brain doesn't know "can't" - it only knows "haven't yet"!
- Here's what makes DELIBERATE practice so powerful:
- Focus on specific skills you want to improve
- Push yourself slightly beyond your comfort zone
- Get feedback and adjust your approach
- Track your progress like a scientist
- Celebrate small wins that lead to BIG victories

Want to turn good practice into great habits? Try these awesome strategies:

1. Start tiny (James Clear's "atomic habits")
2. Stack new habits onto existing ones
3. Track your wins in a success journal
4. Create a practice environment that HELPS you win
5. Build a streak of consistent effort

Let's break down how to make this work in real life:

1. **For Sports**

   a . Pick ONE skill to improve each week

   b . Practice that skill for 15 minutes daily

c . Film yourself to spot areas for improvement

d . Compare today's performance with yesterday's

e . Challenge yourself with harder drills

2. **For School**

   a . Break subjects into bite-sized chunks

   b . Use flashcards for quick practice sessions

   c . Solve extra math problems for fun

   d . Read one extra page each night

   e . Quiz yourself before tests

3. **For Music**

   a . Master difficult passages slowly first

   b . Record your practice sessions

   c . Focus on trouble spots

   d . Increase tempo gradually

   e . Practice with a metronome

4. **For Art**

   a . Sketch for 10 minutes daily

   b . Study one technique at a time

   c . Copy masters to learn their secrets

   d . Keep a progress portfolio

   e . Try new materials regularly

Here's what makes these strategies super-duper effective:

- They focus your energy like a laser beam
- They build confidence through small wins
- They make progress VISIBLE
- They turn practice into a game

- They create unstoppable momentum

Want to create your own POWER PRACTICE plan? Follow these steps:

1. **Choose Your Target**
   a . Pick something you want to improve
   b . Make it specific and measurable
   c . Set a clear timeline
   d . Write down your goal
   e . Share it with someone who'll support you

2. **Design Your Practice**
   a . Break it into smaller pieces
   b . Schedule specific practice times
   c . Create a practice space
   d . Gather needed materials
   e . Plan how to track progress

3. **Build Your Support System**
   a . Find a practice buddy
   b . Join a study group
   c . Share goals with family members
   d . Connect with mentors
   e . Create accountability checks

4. **Track Your Progress**
   a . Keep a practice log
   b . Take progress photos/videos
   c . Note improvements
   d . Review regularly
   e . Adjust as needed

AMAZING FACT: Every single pro athlete, musician, artist, or expert used these exact same principles to become incredible!

So, best to remember these champion thoughts:

- Every expert starts as a beginner
- Progress beats perfection
- Small steps create big changes
- Consistency trumps intensity
- Today's practice is tomorrow's power

Your brain is literally REWIRING itself to become more awesome every time you practice! That's not magic—that's science! And it works whether you're:

- Learning to throw a spiral
- Solving algebra problems
- Playing an instrument
- Creating art
- Building any skill

You've got this! Every practice session is building your path to greatness! Whether you're aiming for the end zone, the honor roll, or any other goal, consistent practice is your ticket to success!

Time to turn those dreams into reality! Which skill will you start improving TODAY?!

BO JACKSON AND JIMMY GRAHAM

Let's step right into the incredible power of versatility—the secret ingredient that transforms regular players into UNSTOPPABLE forces on the field and beyond!

Think about the most amazing football stars who've changed the game forever. They're not one-trick ponies—they're like human highlight reels who can do it ALL! Take Deion Sanders, who dominated both football and baseball professionally. Or check out Patrick Mahomes, who throws mind-bending passes from angles that shouldn't even be possible! These athletes prove that being great at one thing isn't enough anymore—true champions can adapt and excel wherever they're needed!

But versatility isn't about being perfect at everything . It's about building a toolkit of skills that makes you unstoppable in any situation! Like a video game character leveling up, each new ability you master makes you more powerful than before .On the football field, versatile players become team MVPs because they can step up whenever and wherever needed .Christian McCaffrey doesn't care if he needs to burst through the line, catch a pass in the flat, or protect his quarterback—he's ready for any challenge! And Taysom Hill? He switches from quarterback to receiver to special teams like he's changing channels on TV!

But the mind-blowing truth about versatility?

It's a superpower that works way beyond the field! In today's fast-moving world, being able to adapt and learn new skills makes you invaluable everywhere you go .Here's exactly what makes versatility so incredible: When you develop multiple skills, you start seeing connections nobody else notices .A quarterback might use dance moves to dodge tackles or apply geometry to find the perfect passing angle .That same thinking helps you crush it in school, where mixing art into science projects or using sports psychology in group presentations sets you apart from everyone else!

Want to know what makes versatile people so special?

They're problem-solving ninjas! When one approach doesn't work, they've got five more ready to go .They're never stuck because they've built an arsenal of skills to tackle any challenge that comes their way .Think about it like building your own superhero—each new skill you learn is like adding another power to your collection! Maybe you start with speed, then add strength, then develop strategic thinking .Before you know it, you're handling situations you never thought possible!

Ready to boost YOUR versatility? Of course, YOU are!

Start by mastering your core skills—these are your foundation .Then, look for opportunities to learn something new every single day .Try playing different positions in practice .Study how other players solve problems .Mix and match your abilities in unique ways .But don't worry, we'll take an even closer look at these steps in a moment .

Know that every skill you learn makes learning the next one EASIER! Your brain gets better at spotting patterns, making connections, and adapting to new situations .It's like compound interest for your abilities—everything you learn multiplies what you already know!

In the classroom, versatile thinking means you might use sports strategies to organize group projects or apply game-planning skills to tackle big assignments . In life, it means you're ready for whatever comes next, because you know how to learn, adapt, and overcome .

Here are three quick power move examples to start building your versatility today:

- Learn one new skill each month

- Practice combining different abilities in unexpected ways

- Challenge yourself to solve problems using multiple approaches

The most AMAZING thing about versatility? There's no limit to how far it can take you! Every new skill opens doors you didn't even know existed .Every new ability creates opportunities for unique combinations .And every time you step out of your comfort zone to learn something new, you become more valuable to your team, your class, and yourself!

Ready to become unstoppable? Time to add some new powers to YOUR game!

BO JACKSON—EXCELLING IN MULTIPLE SPORTS

Let's crank it up to eleven and take a ride through the jaw-dropping saga of Bo Jackson—the man who obliterated the mold and then built a new one from scratch .

Forget everything you know about what it means to be a superstar athlete because Bo Jackson's story will leave you questioning everything . This guy didn't just choose one sport to dominate—he played *two*, and crushed them both with the kind of swagger you could only dream of!

Now, you might be thinking, "This sounds like some sort of superhero origin story," and you're not wrong . Bo Jackson was a freak of nature, but not in the way you might expect . While others were busy perfecting their craft in one sport, Bo was out there hitting moonshot home runs in baseball and bulldozing defenders in football like it was his side gig .Forget "impossible"— Limits? Bo Jackson was laughing at them .Who else could hit a 450-foot home run and then turn around and sprint past defenders like a human freight train on the football field? *Bo Jackson*—that's who!

Let's talk about baseball first .When Bo stepped into the batter's box, pitchers trembled .His bat speed was so ridiculous that it made pitchers flinch before the ball even left his hands .And when it did? Forget about it .The ball shot off his bat so fast and so far that it might as well have been a missile headed into orbit .But Bo was an absolute *force* in the outfield .He could launch a throw from the warning track that landed at home plate with laser accuracy, and we're talking *on the fly* .Imagine throwing a bullet across a football field, and you get an idea of how ridiculous his arm was .

Bo's athleticism in football was no less spectacular .He ran a 4 12-second 40-yard dash in full pads—that's faster than most players run it in shorts and t-shirts at the NFL combine .You could say Bo was fast, but that would be like calling a Ferrari "decent" on the highway .On top of that, his strength was off the charts .Take one of the most feared linebackers of the time, Brian Bosworth, who had built a career on being *unstoppable*, and Bo turned him into a speed bump, running straight through him like a Mack truck .If you haven't seen this highlight, go watch it now .It's pure athletic poetry .

Bo was an *athlete* .His abilities in one sport didn't exist in a vacuum—they translated into the other .His power-hitting baseball swing helped him explode through defenders on the football field, while his quick reflexes and hand-eye coordination from catching baseballs made him a force to be reckoned with for defensive backs .You want to talk about versatility? Bo Jackson was the human Swiss army knife of athletics .His explosive speed from baseball helped him glide through defenses in football, while the agility he honed as a running back helped him track fly balls like a hawk .

And let's not forget those moments that sound more like myths than real-life athletic feats .Imagine cracking a bat in the middle of a game and still managing to hit a 450-foot home run .

Yeah, Bo did that .

Or how about running for a 92-yard touchdown, sprinting down the field, dodging every tackle, and ending up in the tunnel?

Like something out of a video game, right? Bo made it look effortless .And he was a perfectionist .His training regime was the stuff of legends .Forget the fancy gyms and modern equipment—Bo's secret weapon was good old-fashioned hard work .He ran up hills, practiced his swing over and over and over, and lifted weights that made even the toughest men look at him in awe . His workout was as intense as his game .

But here's the kicker—Bo Jackson didn't even see what he was doing as anything out of the ordinary . To him, it was what he did . He didn't choose between football and baseball because why would he? When everyone else told him he had to pick one, Bo said, "Why? I'll do both ." And he did them at an elite level, simultaneously, with the kind of ease that made it look like he was rolling out of bed and dominating . He would finish a game on Sunday with the Raiders, then hop on a plane to play for the Royals on Monday . No big deal .

Meanwhile, most athletes would be too exhausted to lift their own shoes after such a grueling schedule .

His "Bo Knows" campaign became an iconic moment in sports history because it tapped into the collective wonder of seeing a man perform at such an absurdly high level in not one but two professional sports . The commercials turned into cultural touchstones, and they weren't just selling athletic gear— they were selling the idea that anything was possible if you put your mind to it . Even today, "Bo-like" feats are referenced when someone achieves something beyond the normal realm of possibility . The phrase became synonymous with doing the impossible, and let's be real, Bo Jackson made the impossible look like a walk in the park .

The world of sports culture changed when Bo came on the scene . Before Bo, athletes were expected to pick one sport and dedicate themselves to it . You specialized early, you mastered your craft, and that was your path to greatness . But Bo flipped that narrative on its head . He didn't just carve his own path—he created a whole new highway . He showed the world that being an all-around athlete was not only possible but could be legendary . He proved that you didn't have to choose between greatness in one field and greatness in another—if you had the right combination of raw talent, insane work ethic, and a relentless desire to be great, you could excel in multiple arenas at once .

Even in his downtime, Bo was out there playing baseball because he saw it as a hobby, not something to "specialize" in or to dominate for the sake of a career . Most athletes would be on vacation, or resting, but not Bo . He was out there smashing home runs in the offseason because that's who he was—a guy who didn't know the meaning of limits . His existence shattered the boundaries of what we thought was possible, and even now, the bar for versatility in sports is set by Bo Jackson's example .

But here's the most mind-blowing part: Bo never considered himself anything special .

He didn't wake up one day and say, "I'm going to be a legend today." No, to him, playing two professional sports at the highest level was as normal as breathing .He did what he loved, and his passion for those sports, combined with his unrelenting drive to get better, turned him into a living legend .His legacy changed sports and reshaped the way we think about limits .It was a testament to the fact that greatness doesn't have to be confined to one path or one discipline .You don't have to follow the rules to break the mold—you can create your own .

Bo Jackson showed that you can be legendary in whatever you choose .His story proves that limits only exist in people's minds .The next time someone tells you that you can't do something, channel your inner Bo Jackson .Forget about the boundaries they set .Instead, make your own path .Be legendary at everything you do, like Bo did, and remember: If you've got the passion and the drive, anything is possible .

The world may never see another Bo Jackson .He didn't break barriers—he simply didn't let them exist .And in doing so, he became a legend for the ages, one who proved that sometimes the wildest dreams are the ones most worth chasing .

So, time to stop thinking about the limits and start thinking about what's possible .

Choose to be LEGENDARY at everything you touch!

JIMMY GRAHAM—FROM BASKETBALL COURT TO FOOTBALL FIELD

Talk about a game-changing talent explosion! We're talking about breaking barriers here!

When Jimmy Graham made the leap from basketball to football, he wasn't only changing sports—he was about to change the way the world saw the tight end position forever .

Imagine the scene: A towering 6'7" athlete, once a dominant force on the basketball court at the University of Miami, was now gearing up to break all sorts of rules and reimagine what an NFL tight end could be . It wasn't a change of scenery; it was a revolution in the making . Graham had spent four years showcasing his athleticism and skill in the basketball arena, mastering the art of jumping higher than most players, battling for rebounds, and finishing in spectacular fashion around the rim . He was no stranger to the spotlight, yet as his college basketball career neared its conclusion, something remarkable happened . Despite having one year of eligibility left, Graham decided to step away from basketball, trading in his shorts and sneakers for football pads and cleats . His decision was an absolute game-changer for the entire football world .

The switch from basketball to football was not a simple "switch" by any means—it was a seismic shift that reverberated through the NFL . A player with no prior football experience, who had honed his skills in an entirely different sport, was about to bring a fresh and much-needed perspective to the tight end position . We're talking about an athlete who was a freak of nature, combining size, strength, and agility in a way that no one had seen before . Graham was an athlete who could jump out of the gym, catch with finesse, and—most importantly—dominate with the ball in his hands .

Graham's unique background gave him the type of skills that transformed into football gold . His time spent boxing out players on the basketball court translated seamlessly into football . Suddenly, he was a force of nature that could box out defenders like they were nothing . His ability to position himself and shield defenders came straight from basketball fundamentals, turning him into a formidable opponent for smaller, less athletic defenders .

Graham had a new playbook to learn, but his athleticism gave him the tools to adapt quickly .

His superior jumping ability, honed from years of basketball practice, became the superpower he used to pluck footballs out of the air with an uncanny skill for timing and positioning . He was playing basketball on grass, catching footballs like he was snagging a rebound .

However, it wasn't just his raw athleticism that made him a threat .

The learning curve for Graham was steep, and while it didn't stop him, it required serious work . He wasn't content with merely being the biggest, tallest player on the field . Instead, he dove headfirst into the nuances of football . He treated every practice like a science experiment, trying different methods and techniques to make his skills even sharper . He didn't rest on his laurels . Each practice was a showdown, each rep a chance to fine-tune his craft .He studied film with intense dedication, perfecting his route-running, hand placement, and blocking technique .And when he wasn't on the field practicing, he was in the film room with the legendary Drew Brees, watching tape, developing timing, and learning how to make the most out of every play .

This relentless dedication to mastering football turned Graham from a one-year project into one of the most dangerous and game-changing players the NFL had ever seen .It wasn't long before the New Orleans Saints saw Graham's potential .They recognized that his basketball background wasn't a hindrance— it was a superpower .In the third round of the 2010 NFL Draft, the Saints selected Graham, and that was the moment that would change everything . Drew Brees, one of the most accurate and visionary quarterbacks in history, was about to partner with Graham, a player who had the tools to break every rule in the book .

The partnership between Brees and Graham was something out of a highlight reel .It was electric .While most tight ends were busy running traditional routes, Graham was over here treating each pass like an alley-oop .With his massive frame and incredible jumping ability, he would shield defenders, box them out, and make incredible catches that seemed impossible to other players .

Every time he leaped, it felt like the game was in slow motion .Fans held their breath as they watched Graham leap into the air and snatch passes out of thin air, often turning what should've been a contested pass into a guaranteed touchdown .He caught footballs in spectacular fashion, with a finesse that made defenders look silly .

Graham wasn't using his basketball skills to make only circus catches, though . He had an understanding of space, timing, and positioning that was rooted in his basketball experience .Those years of fighting for position under the basket became the foundation of his dominance in the red zone .Every time the Saints were within striking distance, the defense had one thing on their minds—don't let Jimmy Graham catch the ball .Yet, despite all their best efforts, Graham's combination of size, hands, and elite athleticism made him impossible to contain .

In his breakout 2011 season, Graham stunned the NFL with 1,310 receiving yards and 11 touchdowns, an absurdly impressive stat line for any tight end, let alone one with no prior football experience .He made the transition from basketball to football look effortless . But that was merely the beginning . Graham didn't stop at one incredible season .He continued to dominate year after year, earning multiple Pro Bowl selections, racking up highlight-reel plays, and forcing defensive coordinators to puzzle over how to defend him . No one had seen a tight end quite like him before, and that was because Graham completely reinvented the position .

His rise to prominence did more than change the way we think about tight ends . It reshaped the entire NFL landscape . Teams began to realize that athleticism wasn't just for wide receivers and defensive backs; it was something that could completely alter how a team used a tight end .Graham's success made the NFL take a hard look at players with basketball backgrounds, hoping to find the next Jimmy Graham—a freak of nature who could take the sport by storm .

But while other teams were trying to find their own Jimmy Grahams, Graham was busy putting in the work . He didn't rely on his size alone . He worked tirelessly on his craft, spending hours in the gym, working on his blocking technique, and learning the subtleties of football . His transformation was about heart, work ethic, and a drive to be the best .The result was a player who completely changed the expectations surrounding tight ends .He was a force that could change the course of any game .

Graham's influence went far beyond the field . He sparked a revolution in scouting .NFL teams were looking for basketball players who could make the switch to football and do what Graham did .It was no longer about finding someone who fit the traditional mold; it was about finding someone who had the raw athleticism, work ethic, and dedication to be great .In the years following Graham's rise to stardom, NFL teams began to see basketball players as valuable assets for their rosters, a direct result of Graham's unique success .

The legacy of Jimmy Graham is all about breaking barriers and shattering expectations .

He showed us that greatness doesn't come from following the typical path; it comes from forging your own way, taking your unique talents, and using them to transform the game .What Graham did was bigger than football .He gave athletes from all walks of life a blueprint for greatness .His success proved that with the right mindset, work ethic, and determination, you could take any background and turn it into something extraordinary .

And let's not forget the ultimate lesson from Graham's story: You can take the road less traveled, and with enough dedication and grit, you can blaze a trail that others will follow .

Whether it's in sports, business, or any other field, Graham's journey proves that sometimes the most unexpected paths lead to the most incredible achievements .If you've got the drive to succeed and the courage to take risks, you might end up changing the game, exactly like Jimmy Graham did .

He was a trendsetter, a revolutionizer, and a living example that when you bet on yourself, anything is possible .

LESSON—EMBRACING DIVERSE SKILLS AND EXPERIENCES

BAM—let's dive into something that'll revolutionize how you think about your skills and talents! When we talk about game-changers like Lamar Jackson and Jimmy Graham, we're looking at superstars who didn't stick to one playbook—they created their own!

Think about Lamar Jackson for a second—this guy didn't accept being labeled as "either" a runner "or" a passer .He said, "Why not BOTH?" and turned the NFL upside down! He took his lightning-fast speed, combined it with a rocket arm, and BOOM—created a whole new style of quarterback play that had defensive coordinators wondering what just happened!! And Graham? This basketball-turned-football phenomenon showed us that your past experiences aren't baggage—they're rocket fuel for future success! He transformed those rebound skills into touchdown grabs and those court moves into route-running magic that left defenders spinning!

Here's where it gets extra explosive for YOU—every single skill you're developing right now is another arrow in your quiver of excellence! Playing multiple sports? You're building different muscle groups, developing varied coordination skills, and training your brain to solve problems from multiple angles! Getting involved in different school clubs? You're creating a mental toolbox that'll let you tackle challenges from every direction!

Companies are going CRAZY for employees who can wear different hats! While others are stuck in one lane, YOU can be the MVP who brings fresh perspectives to every project! That drama club experience? It's building public speaking skills that'll make you shine in presentations! That coding club membership? It's developing problem-solving abilities that'll help you crush it in any field!

Let's break down some power moves you can make right now to build your versatility:

1. **Cross-Training Your Talents**

   a . Join clubs outside your comfort zone

   b . Take on leadership roles in different activities

   c . Mix up your study groups to learn from diverse perspectives

   d . Volunteer in various organizations to gain real-world experience

2. **Skill-Stacking for Success**

   a . Combine your interests in unique ways

   b . Look for connections between different subjects

   c . Use technology skills to enhance traditional activities

   d . Apply sports team strategies to group projects

3. **Building Your Adaptability Muscles**

   a . Try new positions in sports

b . Switch roles in group projects

c . Learn from classmates with different backgrounds

d . Challenge yourself with unexpected responsibilities

Now, here's a game-changing truth—every experience you have is building your personal highlight reel! That time management you learned juggling sports and studies? That's leadership gold! The creativity you developed in art class? That's innovation power! The teamwork skills from group projects? That's workplace excellence in the making! Think about the business world like a football field— the players who can run and catch, who can block and score, who can lead and follow? They're the ones who become irreplaceable! Your diverse skills make you that go-to player who can step up wherever the team needs you!

Let's amp this up with some real-world power plays:

1. **In Technology**

    a . Combining coding skills with design thinking

    b . Merging technical knowledge with communication abilities

    c . Blending data analysis with storytelling powers

2. **In Business**

    a . Mixing creative problem-solving with analytical thinking

    b . Combining marketing insights with social media savvy

    c . Uniting leadership skills with emotional intelligence

3. **In Education**

    a . Fusing traditional learning with digital expertise

    b . Merging subject knowledge with presentation skills

    c . Combining teaching abilities with technological know-how

You've got to approach skill-building like a championship season—every practice, every game, every experience adds another layer to your greatness! When you embrace new challenges, you're not stepping away from your strengths—you're multiplying them!

Here's what makes versatility your ultimate power move:

- You adapt faster to change than anyone else

- You solve problems from multiple angles

- You connect dots others don't even see

- You bring unique value to every situation

- You turn challenges into opportunities

And here's the knockout punch—your diverse experiences create a unique brand of excellence that nobody else can copy! While others are playing checkers, you're playing chess, thinking five moves ahead and bringing solutions to the table that nobody else can see!

Want to know what makes employers' eyes light up? It's catching that spark of somebody who can:

- Switch between tasks like a pro quarterback reading defenses

- Adapt to new situations faster than a running back finding holes

- Bring fresh perspectives like a coach drawing up game-winning plays

- Connect with different people like a team captain uniting the locker room

Your future opportunities? They're going to come at you like a blitz package— fast and furious! But when you've got a diverse skill set, you can read the defense, adjust the play, and turn pressure into progress! That's what versatility does—it turns you into a clutch player who can deliver in any situation!

Remember this—excellence isn't about being the best at one thing, it's about being ready for anything! Every new skill you develop, every different experience you embrace, every unique challenge you tackle—they're all coming together to create your personal brand of unstoppable! So take that art class that interests you! Join that robotics club! Sign up for that public speaking workshop! Each new experience is another tool in your toolbelt, another play in your playbook, another step toward becoming that MVP who can change the game in any arena!

Your diverse skills and experiences aren't distractions from your path—they're the rocket boosters that'll launch you to heights others can't reach! When you embrace versatility, you're not spreading yourself thin—you're building a foundation for excellence that'll have success chasing YOU!

That's the power move that'll set you apart—being that player who brings something special to every situation, who sees opportunities others miss, who turns challenges into victories!

THE REAL REASON YOUR HEROES ARE HEROES

"Keep your dreams alive. Understand to achieve anything requires faith
and belief in yourself, vision, hard work, determination, and dedication.
Remember all things are possible for those who believe."
–Gale Devers (Olympic athlete)

There's a reason why sporting legends like the ones you're reading about here are seen as heroes—and as you might be gathering by now, it's not all to do with their performance on the court or field .Whether they're football players, basketball players, hockey players, or soccer players, they've had to overcome some serious challenges to get where they are now .

If there's one lesson to take away from all of these heroes, it's the power of perseverance in pursuing a dream .Most sporting greats have been told that they'll "never make it" at least once in their lives, and without fail, they've picked themselves up and carried on .Every time they're told they can't, they become even more determined to succeed—and that's a lesson we can all take and apply to anything we're passionate about .There's no reason you can't do anything you set your mind to .You just have to be prepared to overcome a lot of obstacles and be determined not to let any failure stop you .In fact, every failure is an opportunity to learn something and train yourself to do even better next time .

If everyone had this mindset, just think what incredible things could be achieved! You can develop that mindset, and these stories are all here to inspire you to do just that. But did you know you could make a difference to someone else's mindset too?

Simply by sharing these stories and spreading the inspiration, you could inspire other kids to chase their dreams with all the passion and dedication of the most successful athletes. One way you can do this is to tell your friends about this book, but you can take this even further by leaving a review online.

If you have an Amazon account of your own, this is super easy, but if not, you can always ask your parents, your coach, or whoever bought you this book to leave one for you. Either way, the word gets out—and that can only be a good thing.

By leaving a review of this book on Amazon, you'll not only share these incredible stories that deserve to be heard, but you'll also inspire other kids to chase their dreams.

Reviews help books get into the hands of the people who are interested in them, and simply by reviewing this book and commenting on a story that particularly inspired you, you'll help other readers find out more about their favorite athletes and carry their lessons forward with them.

Thank you so much for your support. You're making more of a difference than you realize; never underestimate your power!

https://www.champlinks.com/sl/MTE4MzM=/

JOE MONTANA AND BRETT FAVRE

Talk about lighting up the scoreboard of life! When we dive into what makes champions like Tom Brady, Russell Wilson, and Jerry Rice absolutely unstoppable, we're not talking about arm strength or speed—we're talking about what's happening between those ears!

These superstars turned their inner voice into their biggest fan, and BAM—they transformed themselves into unstoppable forces of nature!

Let's break down this mind-blowing truth: Every single play starts in your head before it ever hits the field! When Brady steps up to the line of scrimmage, he's already told himself, "I'm about to make something incredible happen!" That's not ego talking—that's championship-level self-belief in action! Here's where it gets super epic—your mind is like the world's most powerful sports broadcaster, and YOU control the narrative! Instead of saying "I hope I don't mess up," flip that script to "I'm going to show everyone what I can do!" That's not being cocky—that's being ready for greatness!

Let's check out a couple of quick examples of these power moves that'll transform your inner dialogue into your personal hype team:

- **Instead of:** "This test is going to be hard."
  - **Power up to:** "I'm prepared and ready to show what I know!"
- **Instead of:** "I might strike out."
  - **Power up to:** "I'm going to crush this at-bat!"
- **Instead of:** "What if I fail?"
  - **Power up to:** "Every attempt makes me stronger!"

Here's the game-changing truth—champions aren't born with unshakeable confidence, they build it, one positive thought at a time! They turn their inner voice into their biggest supporter, their strongest ally, their most dedicated fan! When doubt tries to creep in, they shut it down faster than a defensive end rushing the quarterback!

Want to see something amazing? Watch how positive self-talk transforms performance:

- Your heart rate steadies
- Your muscles relax
- Your focus sharpens
- Your energy surges
- Your confidence soars

Russell Wilson? This guy turned fourth-quarter comebacks into an art form because his inner dialogue never wavered! When the pressure mounted, his self-talk got even stronger: "I'm built for this moment!" That's the kind of confidence that turns challenging situations into breakthrough opportunities! Jerry Rice didn't become the GOAT by accident—he programmed his mind for excellence! Every route he ran in practice, he told himself, "I'm getting better!" Every workout, he reminded himself, "I'm building greatness!" That's how you turn potential into performance!

Your mind is like a championship team's playbook—fill it with winning strategies and positive plays! When you face a tough situation, your self-talk becomes your secret weapon . Here's a quick power move that'll change your game forever—create your personal highlight reel in your mind! Before big moments, replay your past successes, remember your preparations, and remind yourself of your capabilities! That's how champions stay confident when the pressure's on! The magic happens when you start treating your mind like your most valuable player! Every positive thought is a completion, every confidence boost is a touchdown, and every self-belief is a victory! You're not getting rid of pressure—you're transforming it into power!

Want to know what separates champions from the rest?

It's not talent—it's their ability to be their own biggest supporter! When others doubt, their self-talk gets stronger . When challenges arise, their inner voice rises higher! That's the kind of positive mindset that turns ordinary players into legends!

Your brain is constantly running plays—make sure you're calling the right ones! Think about it like this—every thought you have is either moving you toward your goals or away from them . Champions? They fill their mental stadium with thoughts that push them toward greatness! They don't wait for confidence to show up—they create it through powerful self-talk! You've got a broadcast booth in your brain—make sure it's announcing your greatness! When you step onto any field—sports, school, or life—your inner voice should be your biggest cheerleader:

- "I bring value to every situation!"
- "I'm prepared for this challenge!"
- "I'm getting better every single day!"

Remember this—champions aren't born with bulletproof confidence, they build it one positive thought at a time! They transform their inner dialogue into a force that propels them toward their dreams! That's not positive thinking—that's positive power!

Your mind is your personal training ground for greatness! Every positive thought is a rep, every confidence boost is a drill, and every self-belief is a practice that makes you stronger!

That's your power play for unstoppable confidence—turning your self-talk into your strongest ally, your biggest supporter, your most powerful weapon!

JOE MONTANA—COOL UNDER PRESSURE

Talk about a quarterback who turned fourth-quarter comebacks into an art form! When Joe Montana stepped onto the field, he didn't see pressure—he saw possibilities!

This legendary signal-caller showed us that true greatness isn't about avoiding pressure, it's about transforming it into fuel for something incredible! Let's dive into that iconic moment in Super Bowl XXIII—92 yards to go, 3:10 on the clock, championship on the line .While others might have felt their heartbeat racing, Montana? He spots actor John Candy in the crowd and calmly points him out to his teammates! BAM—that's next-level composure that turned a pressure-cooker situation into a relaxed moment of fun! Montana's nickname "Joe Cool" wasn't some marketing gimmick—it was a superpower that changed how we think about performing under pressure! This guy walked into hostile stadiums, faced bone-crushing defenses, and stared down impossible odds with the same cool confidence you'd bring to a backyard game with friends!

But it wasn't just about staying calm under fire; Montana made clutch plays look effortless .When the 49ers needed a game-winning drive, Montana's heart rate actually went down! While everyone else was feeling the heat, he was in his element, orchestrating masterpieces that left defenses wondering what hit them! That's not luck—that's prepared excellence in action! Montana knew that to truly thrive in pressure situations, it took mental preparation long before game time .His ability to make big plays wasn't some stroke of fate—it was a result of relentless focus and training, constantly visualizing pressure-packed moments and converting them into opportunities .

His mental preparation?

Pure championship material! Montana didn't wait for game day to practice being cool under pressure—he lived it every single day! In practice, he'd create pressure situations in his mind, visualizing every possible scenario until staying calm became as natural as breathing! He turned visualization into a superpower that made real-game pressure feel like a chill day at practice! Think about "The Catch" against Dallas in the 1981 NFC Championship—Montana rolling right, defenders closing in, the season on the line .Lesser quarterbacks might have panicked, but Montana? He stayed cool as ice, waited until the perfect moment, and delivered a throw that turned into NFL history! That's what happens when you transform pressure into opportunity!

Montana's teammates became pressure-proof by osmosis! When your leader is treating the biggest moments like they're routine plays, that confidence spreads through the whole team like wildfire! His calm demeanor in the huddle turned nervous energy into focused determination, making everyone around him believe that anything was possible! And Montana's leadership wasn't limited to only making key plays on the field—it was about the way he carried himself, the way he communicated with his teammates, and the way he handled adversity .

Here's where Montana's greatness hits a whole different level—he prepared for pressure moments way before they happened! During practice, he'd run through every scenario in his head: Down by 6 with 2 minutes left? Prepared . Third and long in the Super Bowl? Ready. Key receiver double-covered? Alternative routes ready . Protection breaking down? Escape routes planned . Clock management crucial? Time-saving plays set .Montana made sure that no matter what came his way, he'd have a plan .

This mental mastery created a blueprint for excellence that changed the game forever! Montana showed us that being clutch isn't about being fearless—it's about transforming those butterflies into formation flyers that lift you to new heights! He didn't run away from pressure; he leaned into it, knowing that each challenge was an opportunity to show the world what he was capable of . This attitude helped elevate him and his entire team, teaching them how to handle pressure situations in a way no other quarterback had before .

Want to see something incredible?

Look at Montana's Super Bowl stats in the fourth quarter—when the pressure was highest, his performance went through the roof! We're talking about completing passes with laser precision while 300-pound defenders were charging at full speed! That's what happens when you've trained your mind to treat pressure like your personal performance enhancer! And it wasn't one or two amazing performances—it was a career full of clutch plays, game-winning drives, and moments that have been etched in NFL history.

Let's break down some of Montana's most legendary pressure moments:

- Super Bowl XVI: Orchestrated a goal-line stand drive
- 1981 NFC Championship: "The Catch" to Dwight Clark
- Super Bowl XXIII: Game-winning drive against Cincinnati
- 1989 playoff comeback against Philadelphia
- Multiple Monday Night Football comebacks
- Countless two-minute drills turned into victories
- Fourth-quarter rallies that became routine
- Game-winning drives that left opponents stunned

This was the Montana legacy: doing what others thought impossible under the greatest pressure.

His pregame routine became legendary in NFL circles! Montana would arrive hours before kickoff, walking the field alone, visualizing every possible scenario. He wasn't avoiding pressure—he was programming his mind to turn it into rocket fuel for greatness! By the time the game started, he'd already played it a thousand times in his head!

He didn't need to wait for game day to get into the zone—he was already there, living and breathing the moments that would define his career.

The numbers tell a story that'll fire you up—16 fourth-quarter comebacks, 4 Super Bowl wins, and 0 interceptions in those championship games! But those stats don't capture the most impressive part—the way Montana made the impossible look routine! He didn't survive pressure situations—he totally owned them! His ability to turn stressful moments into triumphs was the result of hours of mental preparation, unwavering focus, and a relentless drive to be the best when it mattered most.

This high-performance record didn't happen by accident! Montana developed specific strategies that turned pressure into his ally: Deep breathing techniques that kept him centered, Visualization exercises that prepared him for every scenario, Focus routines that blocked out distractions, Positive self-talk that maintained his confidence, Mental rehearsal of success scenarios, Emotional control techniques, Pressure simulation in practice, Recovery strategies for setbacks .These were the tools that allowed Montana to elevate his game when it mattered most, and they can be applied to any area of life .

When other teams were wilting under pressure, Montana's 49ers were thriving! His composure created a ripple effect that transformed his entire team .In the huddle, he wasn't breathing heavily or showing stress—he was cracking jokes and calling plays like it was a practice session! That's leadership that changes the game! Montana made his teammates better with his mindset, showing them that pressure wasn't something to fear—it was something to embrace .

He transformed the atmosphere around him, creating an environment where every player believed they could do the impossible .

Montana's impact went way beyond the football field! He showed us that pressure isn't our enemy—it's an opportunity to prove what we're made of! Whether you're facing: A championship game, A crucial presentation .A competitive tryout .A public speaking event .A high-stakes competition, you can use Montana's mental game plan to turn pressure into performance! Montana's influence has lasted far beyond his football career—his lessons are universal, showing us that pressure isn't something to shrink from, but something to harness and use as fuel for greatness .

Here's the game-changing truth—Montana didn't eliminate pressure, he redefined it! He showed us that those butterflies in your stomach? They're not nervous energy—they're excitement waiting to be channeled into excellence! Those racing thoughts before a big moment? They're not anxiety—they're your mind getting ready to show what you can do! Montana taught us how to use pressure as a tool to perform at our highest level .

Montana's mental preparation routine included:

- Detailed visualization of success

- Physical relaxation exercises

- Confidence-building mantras

- Scenario planning

- Focus enhancement drills

- Stress management techniques

- Performance anchoring methods

- Energy regulation practices

These practices weren't just things he did on game day—they were things he lived, day in and day out until they became second nature .And in those high-pressure moments, when everything was on the line, that preparation allowed him to rise to the occasion .

That's why Montana's legacy isn't about his incredible stats or even his Super Bowl rings—it's about showing us what's possible when you turn pressure into your personal launching pad for greatness! He proved that being clutch isn't some magical gene you're born with—it's a skill you can develop through preparation, practice, and the right mental approach! When you study Montana's game, you realize that staying cool under pressure isn't about being emotionless—it's about channeling those emotions into fuel for peak performance!

He didn't ignore the pressure—he embraced it, redirected it, and used it to elevate his game to levels that left fans and opponents in awe!

Montana's leadership lessons for pressure situations: Stay focused on the present moment .Trust your preparation .Maintain positive body language . Communicate with clarity .Support your teammates .Keep your composure . Execute fundamentals .Embrace the challenge .That's the Montana magic that changed football forever—showing us that when the moment gets bigger, we don't have to get smaller!

We can rise up, dial in, and turn those pressure-packed situations into platforms for showcasing our absolute best!

BRETT FAVRE—PLAYING THROUGHOUT A LONG CAREER

Brett Favre redefined what it means to be unstoppable in the NFL .When he laced up his cleats and took to the field for an incredible 297 consecutive starts, it wasn't only a record—he was destroying expectations and setting an entirely new standard for durability and excellence .

Favre, the Gunslinger from Mississippi, demonstrated to the world that age is merely a number—it was a launchpad for legendary performances .Over the course of 20 seasons, Favre amassed 71,838 passing yards and 508 touchdowns, but these numbers only scratch the surface of what made his career so extraordinary .It was more than stats; it was about the way he approached every snap, every play, and every season with the same passion and enthusiasm as his rookie year .

His career wasn't a series of routine performances .Instead, it was a continuous explosion of excitement, joy, and undeniable energy that ignited stadiums across the country .From his first explosive plays with the Packers to his final throws with the Vikings, Favre made football a celebration . His trademark smile, the one that lit up every locker room and stadium, became a symbol of his unrelenting love for the game .While other players counted down the years and the miles on their bodies, Favre counted his blessings, creating a career highlight reel full of unforgettable moments .

Whether it was his cannon of an arm, which was still launching rockets in his 20th season, his fierce competitive spirit, or his natural leadership, Favre continually proved that age wasn't an obstacle—it was a source of strength .

Favre's longevity in the NFL was a feat that demands a closer look .He turned the quarterback position into an "Iron Man" competition, and he dominated it with style .For two decades, he played through many elements others would find quite challenging but through it all, he remained remarkably consistent, showing up ready to compete week after week .He was a true iron man in every sense of the term, setting a staggering 297 consecutive regular-season starts, and extending that streak to 321 with playoffs included .He wasn't merely a player who showed up—he was a player who thrived, earning multiple MVP awards, countless comeback victories, record-breaking passing numbers, and inspiring teammates across generations . His leadership was about how he carried himself, motivated others, and left a legacy that transcended the game .

Favre's longevity was all about maintaining peak performance year after year .His secret weapons were a combination of passion, physical excellence, and mental sharpness .Favre never saw time as an adversary; he worked with it, adapting and evolving while keeping that gunslinger spirit that made him unstoppable . His passion for the game was evident in how he treated every practice like a championship, celebrated his teammates' successes, and kept things fun even through the most challenging moments .His boundless energy energized his entire team, lighting up locker rooms and inspiring those around him .

Favre's physical excellence was another cornerstone of his longevity. He maintained year-round conditioning to build endurance, recovery routines to keep his body strong, and smart training regimens to ensure he could continue to perform at a high-octane level. As the demands of his body changed over time, Favre adapted, finding new ways to stay in shape and preserve his explosive performance. But it wasn't only about the physical aspect; his mental sharpness played a crucial role. Favre was constantly studying defensive schemes, evolving his strategic understanding of the game, and developing the wisdom that only comes with relentless experience. This allowed him to maintain a competitive edge throughout his career, even as the game itself evolved.

Perhaps most remarkable was Favre's ability to continue setting career records at the age of 40. In 2009, during his time with the Vikings, Favre threw 33 touchdowns and led his team to the NFC Championship game. This wasn't a quarterback who was simply hanging on to his career; this was a player showing the younger generation how it's done, proving that age wasn't a hindrance—it was an advantage! His teammates were equally inspired. Rookies who weren't even born when Favre first stepped on an NFL field found themselves energized by his enthusiasm and passion for the game. He transformed locker rooms into powerhouses of positive energy, where age was irrelevant and the love for football was everything.

Favre's ability to maintain his edge for two decades was the result of consistent preparation, unwavering competitiveness, and a commitment to adapting to new systems. He connected with his teammates, evolving his playing style to meet the changing demands of the game. But through it all, he never lost sight of the things that mattered most—his love for the game, his mental freshness, and his joy in every moment. This ability to evolve and thrive is a key lesson from Favre's career.

He didn't simply survive in the NFL; he thrived, turning every challenge into an opportunity for growth.

His secret to success was in his ability to turn obstacles into fuel for improvement. Favre's approach to maintaining excellence included regular skill refinement, strategic physical conditioning, continuous mental development, and a commitment to smart game management. He knew how to handle stress, take care of his body, and balance his lifestyle to ensure he could perform at the highest level for as long as possible. Where others saw limitations due to age or injuries, Favre saw possibilities .He made adaptability his greatest asset, using every new season, teammate, and system to propel himself forward .

As Favre's career progressed, he changed the entire conversation about what it means to be a veteran player .He transformed the "veteran quarterback" label from a potential limitation into a badge of honor .Instead of slowing down, he became an even greater force, proving that experience combined with passion could create unstoppable momentum .

He showed the world that career longevity in the NFL isn't about hanging on; it's about continuing to push forward, to grow, and to make each season your best .

Favre's leadership lessons are as valuable as his on-field achievements . He showed that age could be an advantage when paired with passion .Consistency, he proved, creates breakthrough opportunities, while enthusiasm has the power to energize an entire team .Experience enhances performance, and adaptability leads to advancement .Favre's resilience built a lasting legacy, and his joy for the game amplified his impact . He proved that durability, when combined with passion, elevates a career greatly .

The numbers are impressive, no doubt, but they don't fully capture the heart of Favre's impact .He made everyone around him believe in the impossible .Favre proved that greatness doesn't have an expiration date .His career is a testament to the power of maintaining childlike enthusiasm, embracing physical challenges, continuously learning, and building meaningful connections .He remained adaptable and open, always preserving his competitive edge while celebrating every moment on the field .

That was the Favre factor—he combined passion with persistence, and in doing so, he proved that age is irrelevant when you approach each day with championship enthusiasm .He didn't fight time; he befriended it, using every season to add new chapters to his legendary story .His lasting impact on career longevity is profound . He redefined what it means to be durable, inspired multi-generational excellence, and demonstrated that sustainable success is within reach for anyone with the right mindset, preparation, and passion . He created a blueprint for how to build a lasting, meaningful career in any profession .

Brett Favre's iron-man career teaches us that longevity isn't about surviving; it's about thriving . Every season, whether it was year one or year twenty, could be the best of your career if you have the right mindset, preparation, and passion . Favre turned durability into destiny, experience into excellence, and longevity into legacy . When you approach each day with a champion's mindset, time doesn't wear you down—it powers you up . And that is the magic that made Brett Favre a legend .

Are you ready to transform your potential?

LESSON—DEVELOPING CONFIDENCE AND FOCUS

BAM—let's talk about something bigger than touchdowns and tackle stats! Your mind is like a super-powered engine that drives absolutely everything you do, and football legends Joe Montana and Brett Favre? They cracked the code on turning mental power into pure gold on the field!

So, think of your brain as the most advanced video game controller ever made . Every button, every stick, every trigger controls something amazing—your focus, your confidence, your ability to bounce back when things get tough! When you tap into these controls correctly, you become UNSTOPPABLE! Remember that feeling when you first learned to ride a bike? At first, it seemed impossible—wobbling, falling, maybe even a few scrapes . But then something clicked, and suddenly you're zooming down the street like a pro!

That's confidence in action, and football champions live and breathe this feeling!

Take Joe Montana—they called him "Joe Cool" for a reason! Remember this? Super Bowl on the line, 92 yards to go, only 3 minutes left .Most players would be shaking in their cleats, but Montana? He looks up in the huddle, points to the stands, and says, "Hey, isn't that John Candy?" His teammates thought he was crazy! But Montana knew something special—when you're confident, pressure turns into pure excitement!

Here's how you build Montana-level confidence:

1. **Practice Until It's Automatic**

    a . If you're learning multiplication tables, start with 2's until they're as easy as counting

    b . In football, throw that same pass 100 times until it feels natural

    c . For a class presentation, practice in front of your mirror until the words flow like water

2. **Celebrate Your Small Wins**

    a . Got five math problems right? Do a victory dance!

    b . Made a perfect throw in practice? Give yourself a high five!

    c . Remembered all your spelling words? You're crushing it!

Now, Brett Favre had this incredible ability to block out everything except what mattered most .Imagine playing football in the middle of a snowstorm, with 300-pound defenders trying to tackle you, and 70,000 fans screaming—and still throwing perfect passes! That's what laser focus looks like!

Try this focus-building game:

1. Set a timer for 1 minute

2. Stare at a spot on the wall

3. Every time your mind wanders, gently bring it back

4. Try to beat your record each day

5. Before you know it, you'll be focusing like Favre!

And here's something mind-blowing—your brain can't tell the difference between something you're vividly imagining and something that's actually happening! That's why visualization is like having a secret practice field in your mind!

Let's do a simple visualization practice right now:

1. Close your eyes

2. Imagine yourself in your favorite place

3. What do you see? What sounds do you hear?

4. Can you smell anything? Feel the temperature?

5. The more details you add, the more powerful it becomes!

6. Use all your senses and fully engage in the moment . You are your own movie director!

Now, let's apply this to football (or anything else you want to master):

- Want to throw the perfect spiral? See yourself gripping the ball, feel the leather, watch it spin perfectly through the air

- Got a big test coming up? Visualize yourself calmly reading each question, remembering everything you studied

- Nervous about a piano recital? Picture yourself sitting confidently at the piano, hitting every note perfectly

Think of your mind like a snow globe .When you shake it up, it's all cloudy and crazy, right? But if you set it down and breathe, everything settles and becomes crystal clear .That's what mindfulness does for your brain!

Try this simple mindfulness trick:

The 5-4-3-2-1 Game

1. Name 5 things you can see

2. 4 things you can touch

3. 3 things you can hear

4. 2 things you can smell

5. 1 thing you can taste

6. BAM—you're back in the present moment!

Putting it All Together: Your Daily Mental Workout

1. **Morning Power-Up**

   a . 2 minutes of deep breathing

   b . 3 minutes visualizing your perfect day

   c . 5 positive self-talk statements (Example: "I am strong, focused, and ready to learn!")

2. **Before Any Challenge**

   a . Take three deep "champion breaths"

   b . Say your power phrase ("I got this!" or "Time to shine!")

   c . See yourself crushing it

   d . Smile—because you're about to be awesome!

Real-Life Success Stories

Meet Tommy, a 12-year-old quarterback who used to get nervous before games . He started using these mental tricks:

- Visualized every play during breakfast
- Did the 5-4-3-2-1 exercise before kickoff
- Created his own power phrase: "Cool like Montana!"
- Result? His coach says he's playing like a different person!
- Or Sarah, who used these same techniques for her science fair:
- Practiced mindfulness to calm her butterflies
- Visualized her presentation every night
- Celebrated small wins during preparation
- She won first place and conquered her fear of public speaking!

Applying Your Mental Game Everywhere

1. **In the Classroom**

   a . Use visualization to "see" yourself solving problems

   b . Practice mindfulness when reading tough material

   c . Build confidence by tracking your daily wins

2. **In Sports**

   a . Create a pre-game mental routine

   b . Use power phrases during tough moments

   c . Visualize perfect technique during practice

3. **In Life**

   a . Stay calm during challenges using breathing techniques

   b . Build confidence through daily visualization

   c . Use mindfulness to enjoy special moments

Your mind is your GREATEST teammate! Like Montana and Favre showed us, the game isn't won just with your arms and legs—it's won with that amazing brain of yours! Every time you practice these mental techniques, you're building your own personal superhero powers .

Start small, stay consistent, and watch as your mental game transforms everything you do . Whether you're throwing touchdown passes, acing tests, or conquering new challenges, your trained mind will lead the way to victory!

Champions aren't born with confidence—they build it, one thought at a time .

THE 1972 MIAMI DOLPHINS AND THE FOOLISH LEAGUE

We're about to check out a story that'll make your brain EXPLODE with the pure, unfiltered passion that transformed football from a local slugfest to a nationwide obsession!

Before the NFL was the powerhouse we know and love today, a group of absolute MAD MEN decided to take on the football establishment itself! These were team owners, yes, but also, they were visionaries who saw a future so bold and gigantic that it made the NFL look like a small, distant relic .And, my friends, this story will leave you wide-eyed, jaw dropped, and ready to charge forward, inspired by their maverick brilliance .

One of the most pivotal figures in this revolution was Lamar Hunt . He was a total football revolutionary and he redefined the game! When he took a long, hard look at the NFL's rigid structure, he didn't see rules to follow, he saw walls to tear down and rebuild into something greater . Hunt understood that true greatness in any sport isn't about playing by the same tired old playbook . It's about innovation . And Hunt, along with other pioneers, would do exactly that . His belief in pushing the envelope and doing the unthinkable led to the creation of the American Football League (AFL), a league that would challenge the NFL head-on and set the stage for the football we know today .

Let's get real for a moment and break down the jaw-dropping stats that show how monumental the AFL was .

Founded in 1960 with eight teams, the AFL soon went on to discover over 100 future Hall of Fame players . Not too shabby, right? But wait, there's more—let's talk about the economic impact of the AFL . To the tune of half a billion dollars in player contracts, the AFL was rewriting the financial playbook, proving that there was room for change and for paying athletes what they were truly worth . But beyond the hard cash, the cultural significance of the AFL was absolutely astronomical . This league was about more than football; it was about the future of a nation, and it played a key role in shaping the sport we know and love .

But why did the AFL matter so much?

These guys weren't here to play nice—they were here to BLOW UP the rulebook! They didn't follow the traditional path set by the NFL . No, they forged a new one, one that introduced dynamic passing games, innovative offensive strategies, and most importantly, contracts that actually valued players as human beings . At a time when the NFL had its exclusive, elitist policies, the AFL opened the door for athletes who had been previously overlooked .

This league was about opportunity . It was a place where incredible athletes, many of whom had been told "no" by the NFL, were given a chance to showcase their talents to the world .

The AFL didn't break down barriers—it destroyed them .

The AFL opened the door for black athletes who had previously been denied a chance to play at the highest level . Before the AFL, the NFL had a history of exclusion, but the AFL changed all that . Talents like Willie Brown, Otis Taylor, and Jim Brown found a home in the AFL, and in doing so, the league became a beacon of progress .It showed the world that greatness isn't about skin color; it's about skill, heart, and grit .

And let's not forget the innovation explosion that the AFL brought with it .The two-point conversion, the rapid development of offensive plays, and electric, high-flying game strategies—these were all born out of the AFL's fearless drive to push boundaries and break the mold .If you could imagine it, the AFL tried it .They were like the Silicon Valley of football—always striving to make the game faster, smarter, and more exciting .The AFL invented new ways to play football, ways that would shape how the game is approached to this day .

They also birthed legendary teams that are still spoken about with awe and reverence .

The Dallas Texans, later known as the Kansas City Chiefs, were among the pioneers of the AFL's success . Owned by Lamar Hunt, the Texans showed the world that you didn't need to be in a major market to create MASSIVE excitement .The team became the blueprint for future team expansion, proving that passion, commitment, and vision could make any city's team a household name .The Dallas Texans, later the Chiefs, were a force, and their legacy lives on .

Then, there were the Oakland Raiders, a team so iconic that the very name "Raiders" invokes visions of rebellious excellence .The Raiders totally embodied football .They created a culture that was synonymous with fearless football, attracting players who didn't fit the traditional mold of the NFL .They thrived on the edge, both on and off the field, and became a symbol of what it meant to be bold, to defy expectations, and to never back down from a challenge .The Raiders were a movement that forever altered the landscape of football .

And let's not forget the San Diego Chargers, a team that rewrote the playbook on offense .Known for their explosive passing attacks, the Chargers showed the world that offense could be as exciting—and as strategic—as a defense .Their unique, high-octane style of play transformed football strategy, and their approach to offense influenced teams for generations to come .The Chargers proved that you didn't have to conform to traditional football structures to achieve greatness .

In 1966, came the moment that would change everything—the merger of the AFL and the NFL .

This was a revolution .The NFL, the very establishment that the AFL had been challenging since its inception, finally recognized the force that the AFL had become .The two leagues came together, combining talent pools and opening up new opportunities for players .The merger led to the creation of the Super Bowl, an event that would go on to become the grandest spectacle in sports .But it wasn't just about creating a bigger game .The merger represented something far more profound .It showed that when two forces join together, the resulting power is far greater than the sum of its parts .

Football wasn't a regional sport anymore—it was a national obsession .

Let's take a moment to talk about some of the unexpected heroes who emerged from this revolution .One such hero was Billy Cannon, a player who, in another time and place, might have been overlooked or ignored .Cannon was one of the many athletes who found a home in the AFL, and his incredible talent helped elevate the league to new heights .The AFL was about giving a platform to the most deserving athletes, regardless of their background or previous opportunities .

It revolutionized the very economics of the sport!

These league founders were economic innovators .They created new revenue streams, challenged existing salary structures, and opened up television broadcasting opportunities .The AFL set the stage for what we know today as the modern sports economy .It was a bold, new approach that transformed sports as a business model and forever altered how we viewed the financial side of professional athletics .

The AFL also kicked off the player empowerment movement .Before the AFL, players were treated like replaceable parts—a cog in the machine .But the AFL changed all of that .The league fought for better contracts, provided medical support, and established retirement programs . The players were no longer commodities; they were respected as human beings, athletes who deserved to be compensated for their hard work and efforts .The AFL helped pave the way for the modern player empowerment movement that is still making waves today .

Strategically, the AFL was a game-changer . They introduced innovative strategies like spread offenses, dynamic quarterback mobility, and complex defensive schemes .The league pushed the boundaries of what was possible on the football field, and those innovations have become integral to the game as we know it today .They created a new mindset for how to approach the game .

The cultural impact of the AFL went far beyond the football field . It broke racial barriers, created economic opportunities, and challenged societal norms . The league changed how people thought about what was possible .The AFL was a cultural movement, a statement that anything was possible if you dared to dream big enough .It inspired entrepreneurs, artists, and thinkers to push the boundaries in their own fields .It showed that sometimes, the biggest changes come from the most unlikely places .

Looking back on the legacy of the AFL, it's clear that there are vital lessons to be learned . The men who founded this league saw it as a challenge, an opportunity to build something greater . They proved that passion beats tradition, that believing in your vision is the key to success, and that every player—every person—has a role to play in changing the world .The AFL taught us that innovation is everything and that breaking boundaries and challenging assumptions is what leads to greatness .

For young fans today, the story of the AFL is a blueprint for how to approach life .

- Challenges are opportunities to create something new .
- Diversity drives excellence, and passion beats permission .

The AFL didn't wait for approval—it went out and made history .And that's the kind of mindset we can all learn from .

So challenge the status quo, and start your own revolution .The world is waiting for YOUR vision .

THE 1972 MIAMI DOLPHINS: A PERFECT SEASON

The Miami Dolphins rewrote the entire definition of athletic perfection . When most teams dream of winning, the Dolphins were busy achieving the IMPOSSIBLE .

Don Shula stood on the sidelines like a general commanding an unstoppable army .At 42 years old, with piercing eyes and a mind sharper than a razor, he was a football ARCHITECT who would design the most remarkable season in NFL history .His players were believers in a dream that seemed absolutely CRAZY to everyone else .

Bob Griese wasn't your typical quarterback .With a cool demeanor that could freeze defenders in their tracks, he orchestrated plays like a maestro conducting a symphony of the most epic moves you have ever seen .When he went down with an injury midseason, most teams would have crumbled . Not these Dolphins .Backup quarterback Earl Morrall stepped in with such precision that the team's rhythm never missed a beat .

The "No-Name Defense" became the most powerful anonymous unit in football history. While other teams relied on star power, these guys operated like a single, ruthless organism. Nick Buoniconti, Jake Scott, and Mercury Morris weren't interested in individual glory. They wanted total team victories, over and over and over. Their season was SUPERNATURAL. Seventeen games played. Seventeen games won. They overcame opponents with a mathematical precision that seemed almost inhuman. Their average margin of victory was a statement. 385 points scored. Only 171 points allowed. These were a declaration of absolute footballing supremacy.

Super Bowl VII wasn't a game. It was a coronation. When they faced the Washington Redskins, it felt like watching a master class in football strategy. The final score—14-7—represented the culmination of an impossible dream.

But here's the most incredible part of their legacy: Every single year since that magical season, the surviving members of the 1972 Dolphins have a unique tradition. When the last undefeated team in the current NFL season finally loses, they celebrate. Champagne flows. Toasts are made. They remind the world that their perfection remains untouched.

This was a group of men who understood that greatness isn't about talent—it's about belief. Unshakeable, absolute belief in something bigger than themselves. Coach Shula transformed a group of athletes into legends. Bob Griese turned precision into an art form. Larry Csonka redefined what it meant to be powerful.

Their "No-Name Defense" proved that teamwork beats individual stardom every single time. They didn't need headlines or individual recognition. They needed only one thing: total, absolute victory. For young athletes watching, their story is about what happens when a group of people refuse to accept limitations. When they decide that "impossible" is just a word invented by people who lack imagination.

The 1972 Miami Dolphins created a blueprint for excellence that continues to inspire generations. They showed the world that with the right combination of strategy, belief, and unbreakable team spirit, anything is possible. Their legacy isn't measured in trophies or statistics.

It's measured in the dreams they continue to inspire. In the young athletes who look at their record and think, "Maybe I can do something incredible too."

Seventeen games. Seventeen wins. One important team that proved success isn't a destination—it's a choice you make every single day.

THE FOOLISH CLUB: FOUNDING THE AFL

They called them the "Foolish Club"—eight visionaries who looked at the NFL's iron-clad monopoly and said, "NOT ON OUR WATCH!"

In 1960, when most people would have run scared, these guys charged into battle with nothing but pure passion and an unstoppable belief that they could revolutionize professional football! Lamar Hunt was the spark that ignited this football revolution .Son of an oil tycoon, he wasn't content to play by someone else's rules .When the NFL rejected his bid to own a team, most people would have walked away .But Hunt? He CREATED AN ENTIRE LEAGUE!

And then there was Bud Adams, another absolute madman of the Foolish Club . A Texas oilman with a heart full of football dreams, he saw an opportunity where others saw impossibility . These were football superheroes who understood that true innovation comes from challenging the status quo!

The original eight owners were a mix of wildcatters, businessmen, and pure football LUNATICS:

- Lamar Hunt (Dallas/Kansas City)
- Bud Adams (Houston)
- Ralph Wilson (Buffalo)
- Max Winter (Minnesota)
- Bob Howsam (Denver)
- Billy Sullivan (Boston)
- Wayne Valley (Oakland)
- Ernest Mehl (Dallas)

They called themselves the "Foolish Club" because EVERYONE told them they were CRAZY! The NFL laughed .Sports journalists mocked them .But these guys? They were playing a completely different game—a game of vision and pure audacity!

Why were they "foolish"?

Because they dared to challenge a billion-dollar sports monopoly with nothing but pure grit! The NFL had controlled professional football with an iron fist, limiting opportunities for players, cities, and fans .These eight owners saw a different future—a future of opportunity, excitement, and true competition!

They were building a revolution! They introduced:

- Higher player salaries
- More exciting offensive strategies
- Opportunities for overlooked players
- Television contracts that brought football to NEW audiences

Lamar Hunt became the heart and soul of this rebellion .When the NFL told him "no," he created an ENTIRE LEAGUE! The American Football League was a complete reimagining of professional sports!

The AFL brought total explosive changes to football:

- Innovative passing attacks
- Two-point conversion
- More dynamic offensive strategies
- Contracts that actually paid players what they were worth

These guys were shattering the rules! They opened doors for incredible athletes who'd been shut out by the NFL's restrictive policies .Black players who were told "no" suddenly had a platform to showcase their incredible talents!

And then came the cultural earthquake of 1966 .That was when the AFL and NFL came together in a historic merger, merging the two leagues into one . This was no mere business deal—it was the culmination of a revolution! The original "Foolish Club" had, against all odds, transformed professional football forever! The merger was the triumph of vision, audacity, and sheer willpower . Bud Adams' Houston Oilers became a testament to their vision .A team that never would have existed under the old NFL system became a powerhouse that changed football forever .The AFL was a MOVEMENT, one that challenged every single assumption about professional sports .

The AFL's legacy wasn't confined to the football field . It shook the very foundation of the sports industry in profound and lasting ways:

- It created new economic opportunities
- It broke racial barriers, opening the door to black athletes who had been sidelined in the NFL

- It transformed sports broadcasting, bringing football to wider audiences than ever before

- It gave smaller markets a chance to shine, democratizing access to the sport

The original eight owners understood something crucial: True innovation comes from those crazy enough to challenge the impossible!

When the first Super Bowl happened in 1967, it was the ultimate validation of their crazy dream! The AFL's Kansas City Chiefs took on the NFL's Minnesota Vikings, and in one of the biggest upsets in sports history, the Chiefs won—proving that these so-called "foolish" guys were anything BUT foolish . The Chiefs' victory in the first Super Bowl was the culmination of the AFL's journey from a startup league to an undeniable powerhouse . It was the final confirmation that the "Foolish Club" had done something far bigger than they'd ever dreamed possible . They redefined football itself!

Their legacy is about believing in your vision, challenging limitations, creating opportunities, and transforming industries .

Now, let's break down some of the incredible lessons we can take from this story:

1. Ignore the Doubters

Your crazy idea might just change the world . The AFL owners were told they were foolish, but in the end, they were the ones who changed football forever . Criticism is often a sign that you're onto something BIG .

2. See Opportunities, Not Obstacles

Where others saw walls, they saw doorways . They created a new future for football . Innovation happens at the edges of possibility, and these pioneers proved that the biggest breakthroughs often come from the most unlikely sources .

3. Build Something Bigger Than Yourself

True success is about collective achievement . The Foolish Club wasn't in it for individual glory—they wanted to create something that would lift everyone up . By building the AFL, they created a platform that would revolutionize the sport and bring new opportunities to players, teams, and fans across the country .

4. Never Accept "Impossible"

Limitations are often just opinions . The NFL said a rival league couldn't succeed .The Foolish Club said, "Watch us ." And they did the impossible .They transformed the football landscape, and in doing so, showed that anyone with vision and determination can change the world .

The ultimate takeaway? The Foolish Club showed that ordinary people with extraordinary vision can transform entire industries! The American Football League's impact was monumental, reshaping not only the sport of football but the entire sports world .It demonstrated that innovation isn't limited to the big players—it can come from the bold, the unconventional, the "foolish" dreamers who dare to defy the odds .

So, what's next?

The world is waiting for YOUR unique vision .The Foolish Club took the reins of their destiny, reshaped the world of sports, and changed the game forever . What's stopping YOU from doing the same?

The power to change the world is in your hands .

So go ahead—be "foolish ." Because sometimes, the "foolish" ones are the ones who change the world .

THE AFL'S LASTING LEGACY

Ready to hear about the most EPIC transformation in sports history? I'm talking about the revolution that was the American Football League (AFL)!

This is the story of how the AFL didn't just challenge the status quo—they obliterated it and changed football forever .So, let's rewind the clock and talk about how the AFL became THE driving force behind the game we know and love today .

Picture it: before the AFL, football was a rigid game .The NFL was entrenched in tradition, and the status quo ruled all .There was little room for change, for innovation, or for players to truly express themselves .This was a time when players were essentially faceless warriors, wearing identical jerseys, indistinguishable from one another .There was no room for individuality, and creativity in playbooks was limited by the unwritten rules of the game .Enter the AFL, bursting onto the scene with a wildly different vision that would turn the NFL's world upside down .

Let's talk about the innovation the AFL introduced .Think about football jerseys for a second .Before the AFL, players wore numbers—but those numbers didn't mean much .They weren't personal, and they didn't reflect anything about the players' personalities .The AFL said, "NOPE, WE'RE DONE WITH THAT!" They made sure players' names appeared on jerseys, ensuring fans could connect with their favorite athletes and recognize the personalities on the field .This was a game-changer in making the players human to the audience .Suddenly, the athletes were individuals—heroes with names, backstories, and fans who rooted for them .

But the AFL didn't stop there . They completely rewrote the playbook by introducing the two-point conversion .This wasn't a small tweak in the rules; it was a bold statement that said, "We're not here to play it safe—we're here to take risks and change the game ."

While the NFL stuck to its conservative approach, the AFL made it clear that football wasn't only about defense and field goals; it was about strategy, creativity, and daring to push the boundaries of what was possible on the field .The two-point conversion became an iconic rule that shifted the game's balance and forced teams to rethink their approach to scoring .But here's the most groundbreaking part of the AFL's influence: the opportunities they created for players .

Before the AFL, the NFL was a closed club .If you weren't from a major college program, forget it—pro football wasn't an option . But the AFL turned that mindset upside down .They weren't looking for players from the biggest schools; they were looking for talent, no matter where it came from .This opened doors for players from small colleges, and even historically Black colleges, who would have otherwise been overlooked .Take Otis Taylor, for example—he came from Prairie View A&M, a historically Black college that many NFL scouts wouldn't have touched with a ten-foot pole .But the AFL didn't care about pedigree—they cared about performance .Taylor's success in the AFL helped pave the way for countless other players who didn't fit the mold .

The AFL broke down barriers!

The league created pathways for communities that had been systematically shut out of professional football .It gave them a voice, a presence, and the chance to show the world what they were made of .And it wasn't only about making football more inclusive; it was about taking down the walls that had kept talented players from succeeding, and putting them front and center for the world to see .The AFL's message was loud and clear: Talent is everywhere . It doesn't matter where you're from or what your background is—if you can play, you belong .

Now, let's talk about THE event that revolutionized football forever: the Super Bowl . The NFL and AFL were fierce competitors, but their merger created the most iconic event in all of sports .The AFL knew they had something bigger in mind . When the two leagues merged, it was a CULTURAL EARTHQUAKE .It changed the way we watched football and the way we celebrated sports .The Super Bowl became the stage where legends were made, where the fiercest rivalries were born, and where fans gathered to witness the climax of a season full of twists and turns! The AFL's bold, innovative spirit turned the Super Bowl into the greatest sporting spectacle the world has ever known .

Let's look at the 1972 Miami Dolphins for a moment .They went undefeated that year—something no one thought was possible .They DOMINATED the season! Every game they played was an emphatic statement: "We defy the odds ." The Dolphins defined what a perfect season could look like . Their legacy was more than a streak of victories—it was proof that, with the right combination of belief, teamwork, and determination, anything is possible . The Dolphins' perfect season wasn't the result of luck; it was the product of a relentless commitment to excellence—a mindset that was born out of the AFL's revolutionary influence .

Now let's step back and talk about the men behind it all . The original AFL owners—what a group of visionary rebels! They were called the "Foolish Club," but that name was earned in the most ironic way possible . These guys redefined what it meant to be an owner, to be a leader, to be a force for change in the world of sports . Men like Lamar Hunt and Bud Adams didn't want to compete—they wanted to change the very nature of football . They wanted to give the game a face-lift, to push it into uncharted territory, and to create something that the world would never forget .

These early AFL owners were mavericks with a vision that was too big for the existing system to contain . They were constantly mocked, underestimated, and ridiculed by NFL owners and traditional media . But they never let the negativity stop them . Every financial risk, every snide comment, every door slammed in their faces only made them more determined .

The AFL challenged the NFL and forced the entire sports world to reimagine what was possible . Their persistence, vision, and unwavering belief in their cause created something truly revolutionary . They completely rewrote the rules!

Let's take a moment to draw some leadership lessons from this incredible journey . The AFL's story is more than football history; it's a blueprint for transformational leadership, and there's a lot we can learn from their approach .

- First, let's talk about embracing your unique perspective . The AFL owners didn't try to fit in; they stood out . They weren't afraid to take risks and pursue opportunities that others couldn't see . Their willingness to embrace what made them different became their superpower . You've got your own unique perspective, too . That's your edge in a world that's often too focused on fitting in . Own it!

- Next, challenge existing systems . The AFL didn't ask for permission to change the game—they just did it . If you want to innovate, you've got to be willing to challenge the status quo . Whether it's in business, education, or your personal life, the greatest innovations happen when people are brave enough to say, "This isn't working—let's do something new ."

- Third, recognize hidden potential . The AFL saw talent in players that others had overlooked . That's a powerful lesson: Don't judge by appearances, backgrounds, or traditions . There's untapped potential all around you—whether in yourself, your colleagues, or your community . Your next big breakthrough might be sitting in the most unlikely place .

- And finally, transform obstacles into opportunities . The AFL didn't let rejection hold them back—they used it as fuel for their fire . Every challenge they faced, they turned into an opportunity to push harder, work smarter, and prove everyone wrong . When you face setbacks, don't see them as failures—see them as stepping stones toward success . Every "no" can become the launchpad for your "YES ."

So, here's your mission, should you choose to accept it: Challenge one of the "traditional" rules in your life, find one hidden talent you've been overlooking, and create one innovative approach that defies expectations . That's how you can start changing your own game .

The AFL's legacy is about vision, courage, and relentless belief . They rewrote the entire playbook for innovation and leadership . And guess what?

You've got that same fire burning inside you . The question isn't whether you can do it—it's whether you're ready to unleash your full potential?

Your revolution starts now!

THE FINAL DRIVE- CONCLUSION

Wake up, future champions! Football is more than a sport—it's a transformative masterclass in turning ordinary lives into extraordinary success stories .

Legends like Jerry Rice, Peyton Manning, and Tom Brady are life strategists who've cracked the code to unstoppable achievement . Their stories aren't about touchdowns; they're roadmaps to personal greatness .

As the quarterback of your personal success playbook, you can think like a leader .A quarterback doesn't react—they anticipate .They strategize .They lead . Tom Brady didn't become the GOAT by accident .He turned every practice into a strategic masterpiece . Where others saw limitations, he saw opportunities . Where teammates saw challenges, he visualized victories . Your academic arena holds exactly the same opportunity . Each assignment is a play, and each study session is a game preparation . You're the commander of your personal success mission!

Football legends never surrender . They never back down . They take setbacks and transform them into rocket fuel for future success . Peyton Manning's story screams resilience . After multiple setbacks, he could have ended his career, but instead, he reimagined his entire approach . He studied harder, analyzed deeper, and worked smarter . Your academic challenges are no different . A tough test isn't a defeat—it's critical intelligence for your next strategic move .

Every struggle is information, not failure .

The most incredible players are obsessive learners . They study everything— game films, opponent strategies, and personal performance metrics . Your education works the same way! Every book you read, and every challenge you tackle is advanced training for life's biggest game .

Motivation strategies that actually work:

- **Build your performance dashboard:** Football players track everything— yards, touchdowns, completion rates . You should create your personal tracking system:
  - Academic grades
  - Study hours
  - Skill development progress
  - Personal growth metrics
- **Design championship-level goals:** Don't set ordinary goals—establish legendary objectives . Break massive goals into precise tactical plays:
  - Specific study time allocations
  - Targeted subject mastery
  - Skill acquisition strategies
  - Measurable progress checkpoints

- **Construct your dream team:** Football is never a solo sport, and neither is success .Build your support network:

  - Find committed study partners

  - Connect with mentors

  - Join success-focused communities

  - Eliminate negative influences

True legends do more than win—they elevate everyone around them .Jerry Rice didn't merely catch passes; he transformed entire team cultures .He inspired everyone—from rookies to veterans . You can do the same . Inspire your classmates .Support struggling peers .Create a culture of collective excellence .

Self-belief isn't arrogance—it's strategic confidence . When others say "impossible," legends say, "watch me!" Their internal dialogue wasn't about limitations—it was about potential .Your capabilities are extraordinary .Your potential is limitless .Your future is completely in your hands .

30-Day Personal Transformation Challenge:

- Identify your unique strengths

- Design a precise growth strategy

- Eliminate one negative habit

- Introduce one skill-building activity

- Track your daily progress

- Adjust your strategy weekly

Remember: Success isn't about perfection—it's about consistent improvement . Small wins compound into massive transformations .Football legends started exactly where you are now—with a burning desire to be extraordinary .

Are you ready to play your best life? Your epic story starts right now!

SHARE THESE STORIES!

Every time you start to doubt yourself or your confidence takes a knock, remind yourself of these inspirational tales .Self-belief is a powerful thing, and every one of these athletes has it .Share their stories now to inspire even more people like you!

Simply by sharing your honest opinion of this book and a little about your favorite story, you'll keep these incredible tales alive, and you'll help other kids find them and feel as inspired as you do right now .

Thank you so much for sharing these stories and leaving a review .They deserve to be heard!

https://www.champlinks.com/sl/MTE4MzM=/

REFERENCES

Adams, A .J .(2013) .Seeing is believing: The power of visualization .Psychology Today . https://www psychologytoday com/intl/blog/flourish/200912/seeing-is-believing-the-power-visualization

AFL History - Origins of the Great Game .(2024, August 6) .AFL News .https://www . bigfooty com/afl-history/

American Football League .(2021, March 5) .Wikipedia .https://en wikipedia org/wiki/ American_Football_League

Augustyn, A .(2019a) .Bo Jackson | Biography, stats, & facts .In Encyclopædia Britannica . https://www britannica com/biography/Bo-Jackson

Augustyn, A . (2019b) . John Madden | American football coach and television commentator . In Encyclopædia Britannica . https://www britannica com/biography/ John-Madden

Babauta, L .(2007) .25 Killer actions to boost your self-confidence .Zenhabits .https:// zenhabits net/25-killer-actions-to-boost-your-self-confidence/

Bankhead, A . (2023, January 15) .Tom Brady: 199th draft pick to the G O A T .The Mighty Sparrow . https://www mightysparrowcoaching com/single-post/tom-brady-199th-draft-pick-to-the-g-o-a-t

Battista, J . (2021, December 28) . John Madden's unparalleled impact on the NFL influenced generations of football fans . NFL com . https://www nfl com/news/john-madden-s-unparalleled-impact-on-nfl-influenced-generations-of-football-fans

Bo Jackson interview . (2024) . Joseph Arangio . https://www arangio com/blog/bo-jackson-interview

Brandt, A .(2016, August 3) .Brett Favre stories from a career with Green Bay Packers . SI; Sports Illustrated .https://www si com/nfl/2016/08/03/brett-favre-memories-green-bay-packers-nfl-hall-fame

Burtaverde, V, Ene, C , Chiriac, E , & Avram, E .(2021) .Decoding the link between personality traits and resilience . Self-determination is the key . Current Issues in Personality Psychology, 9(3), 195–204 .https://doi org/10 5114/cipp 2021 107337

Carol Dweck: A summary of the two mindsets .(2015, March 2) .Farnam Street .https://fs blog/carol-dweck-mindset/

Clear, J .(2014, April 10) .Masters of habit: The deliberate practice and training of Jerry Rice .James Clear .https://jamesclear com/jerry-rice

Clear, J .(2018) .Atomic habits summary .James Clear .https://jamesclear com/atomic-habits-summary

Cotterill, S .T, Loughead, T .M , & Fransen, K .(2022) .Athlete leadership development within teams: Current understanding and future directions . Frontiers in Psychology, 13(PMC8892492), 1–10 .https://doi org/10 3389/fpsyg 2022 820745

David, A .B .(2023, October 11) .Hard work and consistency .Medium .https://medium . com/@adeyemoblessingdavid/hard-work-and-consistency-39e1b38d934e

Davis, J , & Davis, J .(2019) . Jerry Rice's legendary hill training . Stack . https://doi . org/10212950/Stash-Sports-3-200x200

Dianne B .(n d) .The power of inspiration .Expertise .Retrieved November 19, 2024, from https://www expertbase org/a395-the-power-of-inspiration

Durham, S .P .(2020, February 11) .The resilience and determination you have in life . Medium . https://seanpatrickdurham medium com/resilience-and-determination-you-have-in-life-42e325fee521

5 Things to Know: Joe Montana .(n d) .49ers .https://www 49ers com/news/5-things-to-know-joe-montana-fun-facts-nickname-super-bowls-street-catch-wife

Foolish Club .(2023, September 2) .Wikipedia .https://en wikipedia org/wiki/Foolish_ Club

Freeman, L .(2023, January 23) .Embracing diversity and transferrable skills in leadership . Forbes . https://www forbes com/councils/forbesnonprofitcouncil/2023/01/23/ embracing-diversity-and-transferrable-skills-in-leadership/

Frommer, F .(2024, January 15) .Travis Kelce | Biography, age, stats, Taylor Swift, & facts . Encyclopedia Britannica .https://www britannica com/biography/Travis-Kelce

Gagnon-Dolbec, A .(2015) . The role of focus and confidence in high-level athletic performances .Ruor uottawa ca .https://ruor uottawa ca/handle/10393/32980

Gill, J .(2011, February 15) .Great things do happen: The Jimmy Graham story .University of Miami Athletics .https://miamihurricanes com/news/2011/02/15/205553032-2/

Globokar, L .(2020) .The power of visualization and how to use it .Forbes .https://www . forbes com/sites/lidijaglobokar/2020/03/05/the-power-of-visualization-and-how-to-use-it/

Gold Jacket Spotlight .(2024, January 4) .Brett Favre's longevity stands the test of time . Pro Football Hall of Fame . https://www profootballhof com/news/2024/04/gold-jacket-spotlight-brett-favre%E2%80%99s-longevity-stands-test-of-time/

Haycock, K . (2012) . Strategic thinking and leadership . Library Leadership & Management, 26(3/4) .https://doi org/ 10 5860/llm v26i3/4 2635

Health, H .(2018, December 4) .Benefits of mindfulness .HelpGuide org .https://www . helpguide org/mental-health/stress/benefits-of-mindfulness

Holder, S . (2024, September 3) . How tight ends like Travis Kelce helped reshape the position . ESPN . https://www espn co uk/nfl/story/_/id/41017076/nfl-travis-kelce-george-kittle-tight-ends

Houston, A .I , & McNamara, J .M .(2006) .John Maynard Smith and the importance of consistency in evolutionary game theory .Biology & Philosophy, 20(5), 933–950 . https://doi org/ 10 1007/s10539-005-9016-4

How to gain confidence in yourself: 13 tips for self-confidence . (n d) . Calm Blog . https://www calm com/blog/how-to-gain-confidence

Hunitie, M . (2018) . Impact of strategic leadership on strategic competitive advantage through strategic thinking and strategic planning: A bi-meditational research .Verslas: Teorija Ir Praktika, 19(1), 322–330 .https://www ceeol com/search/article-detail?id=772692

Indeed .(2023) .10 Ways to boost your confidence in the workplace .Indeed Career Guide . https://www indeed com/career-advice/career-development/ways-to-boost-your-confidence

Jerry Rice .(2021, February 26) .Wikipedia .https://en wikipedia org/wiki/Jerry_Rice

Jimmy Graham . (2023, March 28) . Wikipedia . https://en wikipedia org/wiki/Jimmy_Graham

Jimmy Graham stats, news, and video .(2024) .NFL com .https://www nfl com/players/jimmy-graham/

Joe Montana .(2020, February 5) .Wikipedia .https://en wikipedia org/wiki/Joe_Montana

John Elway .(2022, February 16) .Wikipedia .https://en wikipedia org/wiki/John_Elway

Knopp, K .C , Rhoades, G .K , Stanley, S .M , & Markman, H .J . (2014) . Stuck on you . Journal of Social and Personal Relationships, 32(1), 119–137 . https://doi . org/ 10 1177/0265407514525885

Learn how effective leadership drives success .(2023, June 1) .Penn LPS Online .https:// lpsonline sas upenn edu/features/learn-how-effective-leadership-drives-success

Libster, M .M .(2011) .Lessons learned from a history of perseverance and innovation in academic–practice partnerships .Journal of Professional Nursing, 27(6), e76–e81 . https://doi org/10 1016/j profnurs 2011 07 005

Lurie, E .(2024) .Harnessing the power of atomic habits .South African Lifestyle Medicine Association .https://salifestylemedicine org/harnessing-the-power-of-atomic-habits/

McGrath, D . (2010) . Joe Montana . Strong of Heart . https://strongofheart nd edu/ profiles/joe-montana-2010/

MD, J .A .(2020, July 9) .Why mindset is key .Age of Awareness; Medium . https:// medium com/age-of-awareness/why-mindset-is-key-f45e602be488

Mehta, mehul .(2023, October 23) .“To put or not to put all your eggs in one basket?” Medium . https://medium com/@mehul96/to-put-or-not-to-put-all-your-eggs-in-one-basket-da3ffdcaa9ce

Miller, J .(2023, August 12) . Council post: The power of diversity and inclusion: Driving innovation and success . Forbes . https://www forbes com/councils/ forbesbusinesscouncil/2023/08/16/the-power-of-diversity-and-inclusion-driving-innovation-and-success/

Morrison, J . (2010, January 14) . The American Football League's Foolish Club . Smithsonian; Smithsonian com . https://www smithsonianmag com/history/the-american-football-leagues-foolish-club-5340540/

Mr .Comeback .(2024) .Pro Football Hall of Fame .https://www profootballhof com/ news/2005/01/news-mr-comeback/

1972 Miami Dolphins season .(2021, March 12) .Wikipedia .https://en wikipedia org/ wiki/1972_Miami_Dolphins_season

1972 Perfect season .(n d) .Miami Dolphins .http://www 72dolphins com/

O'Shea, D .(2016, August 27) .Jimmy Graham: Basketball is his road back to football . FanSided . https://fansided com/2016/08/26/basketball-is-jimmy-grahams-road-back-to-football/

Odell, S .(2020) .Pro Football Hall of Fame Density – AFL vs .NFL .Tales from the AFL . https://talesfromtheamericanfootballleague com/

Oriard, M .(2024, January 10) .American football | Definition, history, leagues, rules, & facts .Encyclopedia Britannica .https://www britannica com/sports/American-football

Pickstar .(2024, September 23) .AFL's impact on the community: More than just a game . Pickstar .https://pickstar pro/au/blog/afls-impact-on-the-community

Positive Affirmations . (2023, November 4) . The power of mindfulness: How it can transform your life . Medium . https://medium com/@positiveaffirmations91/the-power-of-mindfulness-how-it-can-transform-your-life-3e8e21b9eb15

Prosterman, S .(2021, December 30) .John Madden – American cultural and sports icon . Hollywood Progressive .https://hollywoodprogressive com/celebrities/john-madden

Pumerantz, Z .(2024) .The 100 best sports quotes of all time .Bleacher Report .https:// bleacherreport com/articles/910238-the-100-best-sports-quotes-of-all-time .

Quickstart . (2021, July 17) . Why multi-skilling is important in the current world? Medium . https://medium com/qwickstart/why-multi-skilling-is-important-in-the-current-world-6d9e6f7b1042

Raghad Almuntashiri . (2024, March 2) . The power of inspiration . Medium . https:// medium com/@raghad almnt/the-power-of-inspiration-c5d5a895d791

Richards, L .(2022, March 18) .What is positive self-talk? MedicalNewsToday .https:// www medicalnewstoday com/articles/positive-self-talk

Roberts, E . (2023, April 24) . The power of visualization . ILLUMINATION; Medium . https://medium com/illumination/the-power-of-visualization-2b04d753e474

Sarkar, M , & Fletcher, D .(2014) .Psychological resilience in sport performers: a review of stressors and protective factors .Journal of Sports Sciences, 32(15), 1–16 .

Sassi, R .B .(2021, June 21) .Perseverance lessons from 5 entrepreneurs .Medium; Change Your Mind Change Your Life .https://medium com/change-your-mind/5-perseverance-lessons-ef78eca2f8c7

Satterlee, C .(2024) .Casting call: "The Foolish Club" if only there really was a movie about the AFL! Bleacher Report . https://bleacherreport com/articles/623367-casting-call-the-foolish-club-if-only-there-really-was-a-movie-about-the-afl

Scaletta, K .(2010, September 22) .Peyton Manning: Is he the smartest quarterback in history? Bleacher Report .https://bleacherreport com/articles/469822-peyton-manning-is-he-the-smartest-quarterback-in-history

Sports - The universal language . (n d) . Marnie Schneider . Retrieved November 19, 2024, from https://www marnieschneider com/blogs/blog-post-title-one-34l9s

Sutelan, E .(2023, February 1) .Tom Brady's career timeline: A list of NFL moments and records, from draft pick No . 199 to the GOAT . The Sporting News . https:// www sportingnews com/us/nfl/news/tom-brady-timeline-records-draft-goat/ d6xpeqyz844z1aafjdvjr5zoh

The Editors of Encyclopedia Britannica . (n d) .Brett Favre | American football player . Encyclopedia Britannica .https://www britannica com/biography/Brett-Favre

The Editors of Encyclopedia Britannica .(2015) .Peyton Manning summary .Encyclopedia Britannica .https://www britannica com/summary/Peyton-Manning

The Editors of Encyclopedia Britannica .(2019a) .John Elway | Biography, stats, & facts . In Encyclopædia Britannica .https://www britannica com/biography/John-Elway

The Editors of Encyclopedia Britannica .(2019b) .Peyton Manning, biography, college, statistics, & facts .In Encyclopædia Britannica .https://www britannica com/biography/ Peyton-Manning

The Editors of Encyclopedia Britannica . (2020) . Joe Montana | Biography, statistics, championships, & facts . In Encyclopædia Britannica . https://www britannica com/ biography/Joe-Montana

The legacy of influence .(2013, September 2) .AFL Players' Association Limited .https:// www aflplayers com au/news-feed/stories/the-legacy-of-influence

"The perfect season": 1972 Miami Dolphins .(n d) .Pro Football Hall of Fame .https:// www profootballhof com/football-history/the-perfect-season-1972-miami-dolphins/

Tight end Travis Kelce: A game changer in the NFL .(2024, November 14) .Astral Archives Thecmhs .https://www kellymoore com/travel-guide/tight-end-travis-kelce html

Travis Kelce .(2021, August 22) .Wikipedia .https://en wikipedia org/wiki/Travis_Kelce

Trigueros, R , Aguilar-Parra, J . M , Cangas-Díaz, A . J , Fernández-Batanero, J . M , Mañas, M .A , Arias, V . B , & López-Liria, R . (2019) . The influence of the trainer on the motivation and resilience of sportspeople: A study from the perspective of self-determination theory . PLOS ONE, 14(8), e0221461 . https://doi org/10 1371/journal . pone 0221461

Waters, S . (2021, June 9) . The power of positive self-talk (and how you can use it) . Www betterup com .https://www betterup com/blog/self-talk

What is strategic thinking in leadership: Definition, main elements, importance, how to improve it . (2023, June 1) . Lindsay Angelo . https://lindsayangelo com/ thinkingcont/2023/5/31/what-is-strategic-thinking-in-leadership

Wikipedia Contributors .(2019a, February 20) .Peyton Manning .Wikipedia; Wikimedia Foundation .https://en wikipedia org/wiki/Peyton_Manning

Wikipedia Contributors .(2019b, February 20) .Peyton Manning .Wikipedia; Wikimedia Foundation .https://en wikipedia org/wiki/Peyton_Manning

Wikipedia Contributors . (2019c, February 25) . Tom Brady . Wikipedia; Wikimedia Foundation .https://en wikipedia org/wiki/Tom_Brady

Wikipedia Contributors .(2019d, March 21) .History of American football .Wikipedia; Wikimedia Foundation .https://en wikipedia org/wiki/History_of_American_football

Wikipedia Contributors . (2019e, April 23) . Brett Favre . Wikipedia; Wikimedia Foundation .https://en wikipedia org/wiki/Brett_Favre

Wikipedia Contributors . (2019f, October 16) . Bo Jackson . Wikipedia; Wikimedia Foundation .https://en wikipedia org/wiki/Bo_Jackson

Wikipedia Contributors . (2019g, October 23) . John Madden . Wikipedia; Wikimedia Foundation .https://en wikipedia org/wiki/John_Madden

Wood, R . (2010, June) . World's greatest multi-sport athlete . Topend Sports . https://www topendsports com/world/lists/greatest-all-time/multisport htm

IMAGE REFERENCES

Freepik . (2024) .All images supplied by Freepik - Free Graphic resources for everyone . Freepik .https://www freepik com/

Printed in Dunstable, United Kingdom

70342359R00061